MICHELANGELO
COMPLETE EDITION

PHAIDON

LIBYAN SIBYL. Sistine Chapel Ceiling

MICHELANGELO

PAINTINGS · SCULPTURES · ARCHITECTURE

BY LUDWIG GOLDSCHEIDER

MCMLIII

THE PHAIDON PRESS · LONDON

The design on the binding
is a reproduction of
Michelangelo's stone-mason's mark

MADE IN GREAT BRITAIN

BOOK DESIGNED BY THE AUTHOR

TEXT AND COLOUR PLATES PRINTED BY HUNT BARNARD AND CO LTD · AYLESBURY

MONOCHROME PLATES PRINTED BY CLARKE AND SHERWELL LTD · NORTHAMPTON

FOREWORD

IN the course of the last thirty years the Michelangelo literature has increased to a formidable extent. Nevertheless, the most indispensable books have not been brought up to date and we still have to rely on works which are slowly growing old. For instance, we have still no substitutes for the collections of letters published by Milanesi, Gotti and Frey, with their often incorrect dating and their many gaps, while the volumes by Giovanni Poggi of which the publication was announced have still to appear. Nor is there any corpus of Michelangelo's drawings, for that begun by Frey is incomplete and, moreover, as Berenson and Thode have pointed out, faulty from the technical point of view. Similarly, there has been no new concise work containing reproductions of all Michelangelo's paintings, sculptures and architectural works—no unpretending yet comprehensive volume which might have replaced that which was published long ago in the 'Klassiker der Kunst' and rendered good service to generations of readers, but has now become unusable.

In the meantime the quantity of photographic and illustrative material available has greatly increased and the conception underlying it has changed. There exist to-day special publications reproducing all the frescoes in the Sistine and Pauline chapels, with an almost unlimited abundance of details; there are new works on the Medici chapel and the tomb of Julius, with hundreds of illustrations. For two volumes in large format, published by the Phaidon Press during the recent war, new photographs were made of all the sculptures and of numerous details from the frescoes. Use of all these photographs has been made in the present comprehensive volume, but despite this almost a third of the reproductions is based on entirely new photographs, some of them never published before. New, and probably better than any hitherto published, are the photographs of the 'Nicchione'; of the tomb of Julius; of the head of the 'Bearded Giant'; of the Madonna, in profile, from the Pietà in St Peter's; of the St Paul from the Piccolomini altar (after cleaning); of the Bruges Madonna; the Rondanini Pietà; and of the wax and terracotta models in Florence, as well as many others in the Appendix, among them those of the two lateral reliefs in the Moses niche, which have never been reproduced before in any other work.

As regards the reproductions of architecture and the remarks thereon, the reader must not expect to find what he would be justified in expecting in a specialized work (no such work has been published since Geymüller's).

He will, however, find reproductions corresponding to those in the volume of the 'Klassiker der Kunst', some of them replaced by better ones. It must be reserved for a work of quite different conception to include reproductions of designs and ground-plans, together with detailed explanations. Practically all that is presented in the present volume is what is visible to the eye of one who sees the buildings as they are to-day, to the exclusion of what may be deduced from documents and detailed analyses. In exceptional cases, old engravings are also reproduced as quasi-footnotes.

A special section has been devoted to the models, because since Thode (whose judgement in this respect was not so good as in the case of the drawings) they have never been subjected to critical treatment. In order to clarify the problems, a few doubtful items have been reproduced side by side with the ten sketches in wax and clay which after a new and careful examination I regard as genuine.

All the works shown in the present volume I know from autopsy, with the following exceptions: I have not seen in the originals one painting and two models reproduced in the Appendix (Plates XVI and V), and I have not seen the statues of the Piccolomini Altar since they were cleaned.

The textual portions of the present volume are quite unpretending and consist solely of concentrated material out of which the reader may construct his own Michelangelo book. For this reason I have refrained from writing an introduction in the form of an essay expounding my own views and experience and offer the reader in its place an easily readable chronological table which he can consult from time to time if he wishes to refresh his memory with regard to Michelangelo's life and works or the background to some period of his career. The bibliography and the brief notes on the plates are supplementary each to the other, since the notes draw from the works mentioned in the bibliography, and if the reader finds the notes insufficient for his purpose, he can pursue his studies in the works mentioned. The conception underlying the whole volume is that it should serve the reader as a constant companion to the Michelangelo literature, or, in the case of less patient readers, give them, with the choice and arrangement of the illustrations, a coherent idea of the work of one of the most prolific masters of all time.

LONDON: SPRING 1953

BIOGRAPHICAL CONSPECTUS

I. CHILDHOOD · APPRENTICESHIP · BEGINNINGS

1474. The Florentine Republic, during the rule of Lorenzo de' Medici, appoints Lodovico di Lionardo Buonarroti Simoni (1446–1531) of Florence 'Podestà' (i.e. mayor and local magistrate) of Caprese and Chiusi for the period of six months. Lodovico's wife was Francesca di Neri (1455–81). Caprese is in Tuscany, about 40 miles from Florence in the district known as the Casentino, in the upper valley of the Arno.

1475–84. Michelangelo born on 6 March 1475 at Caprese, the second son of Lodovico Buonarroti. (In Florence, the name was spelled Michelangiolo; but Vasari calls him Michelagnolo, and thus the name is sometimes written in the documents. Michelagniolo di Lodovico Buonarroti-Simoni is the correct full form of the artist's name.) When Michelangelo is not yet a month old, his father's term of office expires and the family returns to Florence. Michelangelo is placed in the care of a foster-mother at Settignano (five miles east of Florence), but it is not known how long he remained there. His mother dies when he is six years old.

1485–87. In 1485 Michelangelo's father marries his second wife, Lucrezia Ubaldini (who dies in 1497). About this time Michelangelo returns to Florence to live with his father, stepmother, four brothers and an uncle in a gloomy house in the Via de' Bentaccordi, near Santa Croce. He attends a school kept by Francesco da Urbino.

1488. Michelangelo makes friends with a young painter named Francesco Granacci, who works with the brothers Ghirlandaio. On 1 April Michelangelo becomes an apprentice in Domenico and David Ghirlandaio's workshop. He makes sketches after frescoes by Giotto and Masaccio and copies drawings of the old masters and Schongauer's engraving 'The Temptation of St Anthony'.

1489. Michelangelo leaves the Ghirlandaio workshop (probably in the early part of the year) and enters Bertoldo's school for sculptors. He makes clay figures and a free copy, after an antique model, of the head of a Faun (since lost).

1490–91. The attention of Lorenzo de' Medici is drawn to Michelangelo's talent and he invites him to reside as a guest in his palace, where Michelangelo remains until Lorenzo's death on 8 April 1492. There Michelangelo comes into contact with several leading humanists, among them Angelo Poliziano, who inspires him to make the relief of the Battle of Centaurs (Plate 2); Marsilio Ficino, the interpreter of Plato, and Cristoforo Landino, the commentator of Dante. Michelangelo creates his relief of the 'Madonna of the Stairs' (Plate 1). Lorenzo de' Medici appoints Michelangelo's father an excise officer.

1492–95. Lorenzo's successor, Piero de' Medici, invites Michelangelo to live in the palace again, but gives him only one commission – to make a statue out of snow (January 1494). The spiritual ruler of Florence at the time is Savonarola, whose sermons Michelangelo hears. In the meantime he finishes an over-lifesize marble statue of Hercules and a wooden crucifix (both lost). Florence is threatened by the advance of the French army (entry of Charles VIII into the city, 17 November 1494) and in October 1494 Michelangelo flees to Bologna and thence to Venice; there his money runs out and he returns to Bologna. Michelangelo's father loses his post. Piero de' Medici and his brother flee to Bologna, but return to Florence after a few days. In Bologna Michelangelo sees the works of Jacopo della Quercia and himself makes three statuettes for the shrine of San Domenico (Plates 4–6). At the end of 1495 Michelangelo returns to Florence, where he carves for Lorenzo di Pierfrancesco de' Medici a marble statue of the youthful St John (lost).

1496. Michelangelo makes a marble statue, in antique style, of a recumbent Cupid (lost). This statue comes into the hands of the art dealer Baldassare del Milanese in Rome, who offers it for sale as a genuine antique. Michelangelo tries in vain to regain possession of the statue, which is eventually sold to Cesare Borgia, and was later on in the collection of Isabella d'Este. In June 1496 Michelangelo arrives in Rome.

II. THE YOUNG MASTER

1496–1501. Michelangelo in Rome. He makes a life-size marble statue of Cupid (or Apollo?), which he sells to Jacopo Galli (since lost); Galli also purchases his 'Bacchus' (Plate 7) and obtains for Michelangelo from Cardinal Jean de Villiers de la Groslaye the commission for a Pietà (Plate 11), which is completed in spring 1499. Two years later Michelangelo returns to Florence, where the situation has meanwhile become quieter. (Savonarola burned at the stake on 23 May 1498; the Republic survives until 1512.)

1501–5. Michelangelo in Florence. Contract for fifteen figures for the Piccolomini altar in Siena (5 June 1501), of which only a few were executed (Plates 24–28); contract for the marble 'David' (16 August 1501), which was not completed until 1504 (Plate 17). Contract (August 1502) for a bronze 'David', which was sent to France and has since been lost. Contract for twelve figures of Apostles for the Duomo in Florence (April 1503), of which only the 'Matthew' was begun (Plate 36). A 'Madonna with the Child Christ' commissioned by the Mouscrons, is begun in 1504, but not delivered in Bruges until 1506 (Plate 29). During these years Michelangelo executes three tondi of the Madonna, two of them sculptures and one a painting (Plates 33, 35, 34). Leonardo da Vinci obtains the commission for a mural painting of the 'Battle of Anghiari' in the Palazzo Vecchio, Florence, the left half of the wall being reserved for a 'Battle of Cascina' by Michelangelo, who, however, gets no further than the cartoon; this, too, has been lost and is known to us only through copies (Plate XIV).

1505–8. Pope Julius II summons Michelangelo to Rome. First design for the 'Tomb of Julius'. Michelangelo feels that he is neglected in Rome and flees to Florence (17 April 1506). There he resumes work on his cartoon for the 'Battle of Cascina', on the 'Matthew' and, probably, also on designs for the Pope's tomb. In November 1506 he goes to Bologna to meet Julius (who occupies the city in the course of the war against Perugia and Bologna). Michelangelo makes a large bronze statue of the Pope, which is installed in 1508 on the façade of San Petronio (destroyed in 1511).

III. CEILING FRESCOES IN THE SISTINE CHAPEL ·
   TOMB OF JULIUS

1508–12. In the spring of 1508 Michelangelo is summoned to Rome by Pope Julius to paint the ceiling of the Sistine Chapel. The first half of the ceiling is finished by September 1509. In December 1510 Michelangelo visits the Pope in Bologna, to protest against intrigues. After his return he resumed his work in the Sistine Chapel and finishes it in October 1512. One month earlier the Medici had been reinstalled in Florence by Spanish troops (12 September 1512); Giovanni de' Medici (destined to become Pope in the following year under the name of Leo X) and his brother Giuliano de' Medici (Duke of Nemours) become masters of the city.

1513–16. Julius II dies in February 1513. With the Pope's heirs Michelangelo concludes a new contract for the tomb of Julius. Two statues of 'Captives' are begun (Plates ·121, 124) and work on the tomb continues until 1516.

IV. IN THE SERVICE OF THE MEDICI

1516–20. Michelangelo in Florence, in June 1516 and then again from August on, after spending the month of July in Rome, where he makes a third contract for the tomb of Julius. He becomes the patron of Sebastiano del Piombo, and helps him with drawings for the 'Raising of Lazarus' and other paintings. At this time (1516–19) the head of the Medici family in Florence is Lorenzo, Duke of Urbino, who is succeeded by Giulio de' Medici (later Pope Clement VII). Nevertheless, commissions to artists for the embellishment of Florence are given by another member of the Medici family, Pope Leo X. From 1516 on Michelangelo discusses with him the execution of the façade of San Lorenzo. Baccio d'Agnolo makes a wooden model for this façade after Michelangelo's design, but the latter rejects it (Plate VI-a). Michelangelo makes his own model (spring 1517–winter 1517) and spends most of his time in the quarries at Carrara and Pietrasanta, with

occasional visits to Rome. On 19 January 1518 the contract for the façade of San Lorenzo is signed, but Michelangelo continues working in Florence on the tomb of Julius. He offers to Leo X to execute without payment a Tomb of Dante (1518, Document in the Archivio di Stato, Florence). He gives up his house in Rome and many of his cartoons are burned. In November 1518 Michelangelo begins building a house for himself and his workshop in the Via Mozza, Florence. In summer 1519 he begins the 'Statue of Christ' (Plate 136), commissioned as long ago as 1514, work on a first version having soon been suspended because the block of marble proved to be defective. The second version is completed in spring 1520. On 10 March the contract for the façade of San Lorenzo is cancelled. Work on the tomb of Julius continues during this year. At this point the chronology (cf. the objections raised by Laux, Tolnay and Panofsky, who assume a later date) becomes rather uncertain, but it would appear that the 'Moses' was finished in 1516 (Plate 117) and that about 1520 Michelangelo interrupted his work on the 'four uncompleted Captives' (Plates 127–135). Leonardo dies in 1519, Raphael in 1520.

1521–33. In 1521 Luther (who in 1517 nailed his theses to the door of the church in Wittenberg) is declared a heretic by the Diet of Worms, retires to the Wartburg and begins translating the Bible. The Reformation. In the spring of the same year Michelangelo begins work in the Medici Chapel. In November 1523 Giulio de' Medici is elected Pope (Clement VII). Alessandro de' Medici becomes ruler of Florence. Work begun on the Biblioteca Laurenziana. In 1524 Michelangelo is still working on the models for the sculptures in the Medici Chapel. In 1525 new agreement for the tomb of Julius which is now to be executed as a wall tomb, and not standing free. The 'Allegories of the Phases of the Day' for the Medici Chapel are still not quite finished. In October 1526 Michelangelo sends a new design for the tomb of Julius to Rome. In the following year Rome is occupied by imperial troops under the Connétable de Bourbon, and the Pope, a Medici, is besieged in Castel Sant'Angelo. In consequence, the Medici are driven out of Florence again. Two years later the Emperor Charles V and Pope Clement VII agree to restore Alessandro. In 1529 Michelangelo is employed mainly as a military engineer, fortifying Florence against attacks by the Medici in their attempts to return. Michelangelo lends the city a thousand scudi. He goes to Ferrara to ask the Duke for advice concerning fortifications, promises him a picture and paints 'Leda and the Swan'. The picture (afterwards lost in France) is not delivered, but presented to Mini, Michelangelo's favourite pupil. In September 1529 Michelangelo returns to Florence, but in the same month flees to Ferrara and thence to Venice. He is declared a traitor and threatened with confiscation of his property, whereupon he returns to Florence while the city is besieged. On 12 August 1530 Florence

Jonah. Detail of Plate 109.

capitulates and the imperial troops enter the city, which is handed over to Clement VII, who appoints Baccio Valori his commissary. Michelangelo remains in hiding, but is promised immunity by the Pope if he will continue his work on the Medici Chapel. In the autumn of the same year he resumes work in the Chapel and presents Baccio Valori with an 'Apollo' (Plate 175). During this disturbed period Michelangelo's father dies (not in 1534, as at one time was supposed). The reliquary loggia in San Lorenzo completed in 1532 (Plate 140). On 29 April of the same year, fourth contract for the tomb of Julius.

V. TRANSITIONS

1533–34. Michelangelo spends the winter 1532–33 in Rome. He forms a lifelong friendship with Tommaso de' Cavalieri, to whom he dedicates many poems and drawings. He decides to settle in Rome. In June 1533 he returns for three months to Florence. At that time the 'Allegories of the Phases of the Day' were still lying on the floor of the Medici Chapel, but shortly before Michelangelo's final move to Rome, at least the statues of the two Medici Dukes had been installed in their niches. From November 1533 to May 1534 Michelangelo is in Rome, where he receives from the Pope the commission for the 'Last Judgement' and works once more on the tomb of Julius. After this he again spends three months in Florence and the benches and the wooden ceiling of the Biblioteca Laurenziana,

designed as long ago as 1526, are now completed (Plates VI and VII). Assistants carry on the work on the Laurenziana and after many interruptions it is at last finished in 1559, when Ammanati and Vasari execute the staircase after drawings and a model by Michelangelo (Plate 142). The Medici Chapel is also left unfinished after Michelangelo's departure and the remaining work is entrusted to assistants (see, e.g., Plate IV).

In September 1534 Michelangelo moves to Rome and does not return to Florence during the remaining thirty years of his life. The Medici remain rulers of the city; first Alessandro, and then, after his murder (1537), Cosimo I, both of whom are disliked by Michelangelo, who refuses all the flattering offers of the Grand Duke.

VI. THE 'LAST JUDGEMENT'

1534–41. Two days after Michelangelo's arrival in Rome, on 25 September 1534, Pope Clement VII dies and is succeeded by Alessandro Farnese (Paul III). Michelangelo, who wants to continue work on the tomb of Julius, is ordered by the new Pope to begin the altarpiece for the Sistine Chapel, the 'Last Judgement'. The preparatory work lasts until 1536 and the fresco is completed in 1541. Friendship with Vittoria Colonna (from 1538), for whom Michelangelo makes a 'Crucifixion' and other religious drawings. He comes into contact with Cardinal Pole and the religious circle of the 'spirituali'. In 1538 Ignatius Loyola comes to Rome; Michelangelo's conversations with Francisco de Hollanda.

VII. RELIGIOUS THEMES

1542–45. First fresco in the Cappella Paolina, the 'Conversion of St Paul', commissioned by Pope Paul III (Plate 193). At the same time, after forty years' work, the tomb of Julius is completed (Plate 188). On 8 January 1544 (according to the Florentine calendar, =1545), death at the age of fifteen of Cecchino Bracci, nephew and favourite of Luigi del Riccio, one of Michelangelo's friends. Michelangelo composes fifty poetical inscriptions and makes a drawing for the boy's tomb, which is executed by Francesco Urbino (Plate XII-a). In November 1545 Pietro Aretino attacks Michelangelo in an open letter for his 'godlessness' and blames him for the unseemliness of the many nudes in the 'Last Judgement'. The first Council of Trent begins its sittings. The Counter-Reformation.

1546. Antonio da Sangallo dies and Michelangelo takes over the construction of the Palazzo Farnese, at the same time making the first designs for the decoration of the Capitol and beginning his share in the work of building St Peter's (Plates 200–208; 218–223).

1546–50. Second fresco in the Cappella Paolina, the 'Crucifixion of St Peter' (Plate 194). First plans for the reconstruction of San Giovanni dei Fiorentini in Rome (on which Michelangelo works until 1560). The first edition of Vasari's 'Vite' is published, including the biography of Michelangelo (1550). In the same year appear Benedetto Varchi's 'Due Lezioni' on Michelangelo as a poet.

VIII. THE LAST PHASE

1551–64. In 1553, execution of the floor of the Biblioteca Laurenziana (Plate VII-b), in imitation of the carved ceiling. Publication of Ascanio Condivi's 'Vita di Michelangelo'. At the end of 1555, death of Michelangelo's servant and assistant, Francesco Urbino, who served him for twenty-five years. Shortly before this Michelangelo damages with blows of his hammer the 'Florentine Pietà' (Plate 210), which Tiberio Calcagni subsequently restores. Michelangelo begins the 'Palestrina Pietà' (Plate 213), which is completed by another hand. He also begins the 'Rondanini Pietà', on which he himself works until his death (Plate 214). Production of important religious drawings, especially 'Crucifixions'. In 1558 Michelangelo makes a model for the staircase of the Laurenziana (Plates 142, 143), and begins his model for the dome of St Peter's, which he finishes in 1561 (Plate 223). About the same time Michelangelo works on the project for the transformation of the Thermae of Diocletian into the church of Santa Maria degli Angeli (Plate XI), the designs for the outer side of the Porta Pia (Plate 217) and for the Sforza Chapel in Santa Maria Maggiore (Plate XII-b, c). On 12 February 1564 Daniele da Volterra watches the master working all day long on a 'Pietà'. Two days later Michelangelo falls ill and, though feverish, wanders about in the open air, telling his assistant Calcagni that he can find no rest. The following day, as he is still more feverish, he remains by the fireside. After only two days in bed, he dies on 18 February 1564, in the presence of Tommaso de' Cavalieri, Daniele da Volterra and a number of doctors and friends. The body is taken to the church of the Santi Apostoli and the Pope wishes it to be buried in St Peter's, but Michelangelo's nephew and heir, Leonardo, secretly removes coffin and body to Florence. The dead master arrives in his native city on 10 March and is buried in Santa Croce, but the solemn commemoration is not held until 14 July, in San Lorenzo. More than a hundred artists are present and the funeral oration is spoken by Benedetto Varchi. The Grand Duke was not present. (Shakespeare was born a few weeks after Michelangelo's death.)

The 'Nicchione' of the Belvedere. Detail of an engraving, 1574 (cf. Plate 209).

MADONNA DONI. Florence, Uffizi

CATALOGUE

MADONNA OF THE STAIRS. Plate 1. Marble relief, 22 × 15¾ in. Executed c. 1491, when the artist was about sixteen years old. First mentioned by Vasari in the second edition of his *Lives* (1568) and described by him as being not quite one (Florentine) ell[1] in height and the 'only bas-relief' by Michelangelo. According to Vasari, it then belonged to Leonardo Buonarroti, Michelangelo's nephew. It subsequently came into the possession of the Medici, who in 1617 presented it to the Casa Buonarroti. Since Vasari's day its relationship to reliefs by Donatello has often been stressed, notably by Bode. The attribution to Michelangelo has, without adequate reason, been doubted by Charles Holroyd (1911) and Ernst Benkard (1933).

BATTLE OF CENTAURS. Plate 2 (3). Marble relief, 33¼ × 35⅝ in. Vasari (1568) calls it 'a battle between Hercules and the Centaurs', while Condivi (1553) describes it as 'the Rape of Dejanira and the battle of Centaurs'.[2] According to Condivi, the idea of this relief was suggested to Michelangelo by Poliziano (died 1494), the tutor of Lorenzo il Magnifico's sons. The poet and humanist Poliziano may have derived his knowledge of the subject from Boccaccio's *Genealogia* or from the collection of legends attributed to Hyginus. The individual figures in this relief have little material clarity; it is hard to decide which of them are Centaurs, and still more difficult to distinguish males from females. Wölfflin maintained that there was not a single female figure in the relief, whereas Symonds believed that the central figure was female. According to Justi, however, this central figure is the Centaur Eurytion, while Knapp thinks it is either Hercules or Theseus. The representation is modelled on sarcophagus fronts of the Roman Imperial period, and Bertoldo's equestrian relief has rightly been compared with it. Michelangelo seems to have been very fond of his Centaur relief, which he executed when he was seventeen (his fondness for it is confirmed by Condivi); in any case he kept it all his life, and it then passed into the possession of his family.

THE THREE BOLOGNA STATUETTES. Plates 4–6. Marble; Proculus, 22 in.; Petronius, 25 in.; the angel, 20¼ in. high, with base. Condivi mentions only the *Petronius* and the *Angel holding a candlestick* and says that Michelangelo received 18 ducats for the Saint and 12 for the angel. According to C. Gnudi (1942) and Bertini (1945), the *Petronius* was begun by Niccolò dell' Arca and finished by Michelangelo, who left the back of the statue as he found it. This opinion is based on a statement by Lodovico da Prelormo (1572), but Tolnay declared the statuette to be 'entirely by the hand of the Master'. The *Proculus*, 'the most interesting of the three figures' (Johannes Wilde), is first mentioned, together with the other two, by Leandro Alberti in his '*De divi Dominici obitu*

et sepultura' (1535). 'Foratti questions the authenticity of the Proculus, which it is true one would not be sorry to see eliminated from Michelangelo's œuvre, but on the other hand it is too well authenticated by Fra Lodovico da Prelormo and Leandro Alberti to justify its arbitrary rejection' (Panofsky). In addition to Foratti, Wölfflin and Frey have declared themselves against the attribution of the Proculus to Michelangelo; Thode, Mackowsky and Bode have given excellent reasons in favour of its authenticity. According to contemporary reports, the statue was knocked down and broken in 1572 while it was being cleaned; the shanks were broken off and it is still easy to see where they were stuck on again. Thode thought: 'In my opinion there can be no doubt that in the Proculus we have a self-portrait of the nineteen-year-old artist.' Michelangelo's angel is the male counterpart of the delicate female angel by Niccolò dell' Arca, who executed the rest of the decoration over the shrine of St Dominic. Justi summed up the figures: 'The three Bologna statuettes – the fruits of one year's sojourn in the city – are probably the most insignificant and least satisfactory works which have been handed down to us under Michelangelo's name, but it must be admitted that they are only too well authenticated.' On the other hand, Stendhal says in their favour: 'These figures are remarkable, one sees quite clearly that this great artist began by imitating nature in the most painstaking way and that he knew how to render all her charm and *morbidezza*.' (See also Malvasia, *Le Pitture di Bologna*, third edition, p. 246.)

BACCHUS. Plate 7 (8–10). Marble, 80 in. high, including base. According to Condivi, executed for the Roman banker Jacopo Galli in his house. Commissioned in 1496; intended for erection in a garden. The Bacchus and Satyr are hewn out of one block. Vasari was the first to notice the hermaphroditic element in the figure: 'A marvellous blending of both sexes – combining the slenderness of a youth with the round fullness of a woman'; to which Condivi adds: 'The eyes are weak and lewd.' The pathological character of the figure has often repelled critics. Brinckmann calls it 'the coarsest work by Michelangelo which we possess'; Mackowsky describes the 'vice in a beaming youthful countenance' as an aesthetic error. Stendhal remarks: 'Michelangelo divined the antique, in so far as it expresses strength, but the face is coarse and without charm.' Similarly the poet Shelley wrote: 'The countenance of this figure is the most revolting mistake of the spirit and meaning of Bacchus. It looks drunken, brutal and narrow-minded, and has an expression of dissoluteness the most revolting.' He finds fault with the stiffness of the legs, quite wrongly, for they are a naturalistic rendering of the semi-paralysed movements of the drunken god. All critics note the artistic perfection of the carving and the Christian element in this pagan theme. Michelangelo treated the subject again in a more clearly comprehensible manner in his *Drunkenness of Noah* in the frescoes of the Sistine Chapel; and again in the presentation drawing for Cavalieri, *A Bacchanal of Children*. In all three cases the power of sin is depicted – in the shape of drunkenness.

---

[1] A Florentine ell = 23 in.
[2] There is a detailed study of the subject-matter in Tolnay, I 133. Wickhoff suggested that the correct title should be: 'The Marriage of Deidameia and Battle between Centaurs and Lapithae'. Theseus and Hercules are fighting on the side of the Lapithae.

9

MICHAEL·AGELVS·BONAROTVS·FLOREN·FACIEBAT

Michelangelo's signature on the Pietà at St Peter's

PIETÀ (Madonna della Febbre). Plate 11 (12–16). Marble, 69 in. high. The only work by Michelangelo bearing his genuine signature. The group was commissioned by Cardinal Jean de Villiers de la Groslaye (died 1499), French Ambassador to the Holy See. The contract was made on 27 August 1498, the price agreed upon being 450 ducats. The chief work of Michelangelo's youthful period. The subject was a complete novelty for Italy – at least as far as sculpture is concerned,[3] and many of Michelangelo's contemporaries considered it heretical; an orthodox writer of 1549 describes it as a 'Lutheran notion'. Michelangelo's Pietà originally stood in the Petronilla chapel, the so-called French chapel of the old church of St Peter's; after the demolition of the latter about 1535, it was installed in the new St Peter's, at first in the Cappella della Febbre, the 'fever chapel'. Since 1749 it has been in the Cappella del Crocifisso (Cappella della Pietà).

DAVID ('The Giant'). Plate 17 (18–23). Marble, 14 ft. 3 in. high, including base. The contract between the Operai of the Cathedral and Michelangelo is dated 16 August 1501, with a term of delivery of two years and a fee which was subsequently raised to 400 ducats. On 25 January 1504 a conference of artists was held, to decide where the David should be erected; among the participants were Leonardo da Vinci, Botticelli, Filippino Lippi, Perugino and Piero di Cosimo. It was resolved that Donatello's Judith should be removed from the entrance to the Palazzo Vecchio, in order to make room for Michelangelo's David. On 8 September 1504 the erection in front of the Palazzo Vecchio was completed. In 1873 the statue was removed to the Accademia and a marble replica was placed in front of the Palazzo Vecchio. Michelangelo was given a block of marble out of which Agostino di Duccio, or perhaps Baccellino, had attempted to hew a David. 'So Michelangelo made a wax model of a youthful David holding the sling, which might serve as the emblem of the palace' (Vasari). When the Medici were driven out of Florence on 26 April 1527, the statue was damaged by a bench thrown out of one of the palace windows and the left arm was shattered. The three pieces were found by Salviati and Vasari and in 1543; by order of Duke Cosimo, they were replaced. Burckhardt finds fault with the 'preoccupation with the model' seen in this statue and with the 'mistake' of trying to represent the figure of an adolescent in colossal proportions. 'Only grown persons can be conveniently enlarged. . . . When seen through a diminishing glass, the David gains uncommonly in beauty and life; to be sure with exception of

the head, which seems to have been designed for quite a different mood.' On the other hand Justi writes: 'His most perfect statue of a nude man, considered from a purely technical and plastic standpoint as life in marble.'

FIVE STATUES OF THE PICCOLOMINI ALTAR, SIENA CATHEDRAL. Plates 24–28. Marble, each about 50 in. high. Cardinal Francesco Piccolomini, later Pope Pius III, ordered the altar from the Lombard sculptor Andrea Bregno, who erected it in 1481–5. Sixteen statues were to decorate this altar, and in 1501 (when Bregno was eighty), the Cardinal approached Pietro Torrigiano, who began the figure of St Francis (Plate 26), but did not finish it. In the same year the commission was offered to Michelangelo, who first finished Torrigiano's St Francis, and then, between June 1501 and October 1504, delivered four more statues (Plates 24, 25, 27, 28). The contract was renewed in 1504. Valentiner believes that the Bruges Madonna (Plate 29) was originally intended for the upper central niche of this altar. St Peter and St Paul were of course meant as counterpieces, and in 1944 they were placed accordingly: St Peter in the lower right niche, St Paul in the lower left niche. St Francis, previously in the place of St Paul, was moved to the upper left niche. St Gregory and St Pius, also counterpieces, have always rightly been placed in the middle niches.[4] Burckhardt (1891), Thode (1908), J. Wilde (1932), Toesca (1934), F. Kriegbaum (1941), Valentiner (1942), and A. Bertini (1945) have accepted the statues as Michelangelo's own work. Tolnay (1947 and 1951) insists that the execution is due mainly to Baccio da Montelupo. According to Kriegbaum, the St Paul (Plate 28) is a self-portrait of Michelangelo (who at that time was about twenty-seven).

Michelangelo's sketch of a marble block with measurements and his stone-mason's mark. (Pen and ink drawing. Formerly Collection Stefan Zweig.)

THE BRUGES MADONNA. Plate 29 (30–32). Marble, 50½ in. high, including base. The earliest mention of this work occurs in Albrecht Dürer's diary of his journey to the Netherlands, on 7 April 1521: 'Then I saw the alabaster likeness of Mary in Our Lady, which was made by

---

[3] There is a clear relationship, not confined merely to the choice of subject, to the Lamentation of Christ by Jacopo del Sellaio (1442–93), now in the Berlin Museum (Cat. No. 1055), especially as regards the pathetic opening of the Madonna's hand and the pendent right arm of the Christ. As this painting probably came from the church of San Frediano in Florence, it may well have been familiar to Michelangelo. The date of Sellaio's painting is 1483; Leonardo's Christ in 'The Last Supper' imitates the gestures of Sellaio's Madonna.

[4] Kriegbaum calls the 'bishop' St Pius, and the 'pope' St Gregory; but our captions follow Valentiner (1950) and Tolnay (1947).

Michael Angelo of Rome.' (Alabaster here means white marble, and Our Lady is Durer's way of saying 'Notre-Dame'.) Condivi, who never saw the work, which Francesco del Pugliese brought to Bruges in 1506, describes it as a bronze,[5] and says that the Bruges merchant Mouscron[6] paid 100 ducats for it.[7] The French sculptor David d'Angers claimed to have discerned the hand of an assistant; Wölfflin was of the same opinion. Pieraccini, in his guide to the Tribuna del David (Prato, 1883) includes it among the 'doubtful works'. Apparently the group is designed to be placed rather high. In the present position the head of the Child seems too large.[8]

THE ROUND MADONNA RELIEF IN FLORENCE. Plate 33. Marble, 33½ in. Also known as the Pitti Madonna, after Bartolommeo Pitti, who commissioned it. Executed at about the same time as the other two round Madonnas, the *Taddei Madonna* in London (Plate 35) and the tempera painting, the *Doni Madonna* in Florence (Plate 34). Justi stresses the intimate character of the work and the fact that it was intended 'for the home' and 'not for oratories or tombs'. At one time the relief was considered to be 'unfinished', but to modern eyes this does not seem to be the case.

THE HOLY FAMILY. Plate 34. Wood, resin and tempera.[9] Diameter 47¼ in. Known as the 'Doni Madonna', after Angelo Doni, who commissioned the work. The only certain easel painting by Michelangelo, but at the same time the least esteemed of his paintings. Even Doni seems to have been dissatisfied with it, for Vasari tells us of a long dispute about the fee. The picture was subsequently taken out of its original frame and a tondo by Lorenzo di Credi was put in its place.[10]

Stendhal thought that the task was unworthy of Michelangelo: 'A Hercules sewing petticoats.' Art historians of the late nineteenth century were unanimous in their disapproval of the Doni Madonna. 'With sentiments of this kind nobody ought to paint a Holy Family', was Burckhardt's opinion, and he also discovered 'deliberate difficulties' in it. Justi considered it temperamental: 'The play of the arrangement of the limbs ruins the impression; the idyll of parental felicity becomes a gymnastic exercise.' Nevertheless, the picture is a miracle of draughtsmanship and powerful composition, merits which perhaps only painters are capable of appreciating. The colours would have aroused the enthusiasm of Ingres. The work contains the germ of everything which makes the ceiling of the Sistine Chapel unique, even the superabundance of muscles. This Madonna is a sister of the Delphic Sibyl; the youth half concealed by Joseph's shoulder is a fore-runner of one of the nudes of the Sistine ceiling (Plate 70). When we remember that an interval of less than four years separates the 'Doni Madonna' from the ceiling paintings of the Sistine Chapel, we realize the fantastic strides which Michelangelo made in the course of his career.

THE ROUND MADONNA RELIEF IN LONDON. Plate 35. Marble, 43 in. Also known as the Taddei Madonna, after its first owner, Taddeo Taddei. Thode and Wölfflin think that the Pitti Madonna is the older of the two, but Knapp and others consider the Taddei tondo to be the older. The relief is held to be unfinished and a number of opinions concerning its sketchiness were collected by Justi (II, p. 190). Walter Pater wrote of it: 'Michelangelo secures that ideality of expression which in Greek sculpture depends on a delicate system of abstraction, and in early Italian sculpture on lowness of relief, by an incompleteness, which is surely not always undesigned, and which trusts to the spectator to complete the half-emergent form.' Within Michelangelo's œuvre these two round reliefs represent his 'small sculptures'. Justi stresses the 'genre-like' treatment of the Taddei Madonna and the fact that it was 'intended for a room in a bourgeois home'.
The Taddei Madonna was bought in 1822 by Sir George Beaumont in Rome, and after his death, and the death of his wife, it was presented to the Royal Academy (1830).[11]

ST MATTHEW. Plate 36. Marble, 8 ft. 11 in. Unfinished. Begun immediately after the David, a contract having been signed on 24 April 1503 with the Arte della Lana in Florence for twelve Apostles for the Cathedral. In the winter of 1504-5 Michelangelo was working mainly on his battle cartoon; in March 1505 he was summoned to Rome by Julius II, with whom he made a five-year contract for the tomb. After this, on 18 December 1505, the contract for the Apostles was cancelled. Four months later, when Michelangelo fled from Rome to Florence, he appears to have resumed work on the St Matthew (April–November 1506). At the end of

---

[5] Vasari calls it a 'bronze tondo'. Considering that Condivi wrote under Michelangelo's eyes, one cannot simply assume that he certainly made a mistake. Valentiner (*Art Quarterly*, 1942) showed the possibility that the Bruges Madonna was originally intended for the Piccolomini altar, and therefore it is not impossible that Mouscron bought from Michelangelo also a bronze tondo, perhaps similar in style to the two marble tondi, Plates 33 and 35. Benedetto Varchi, in his funeral oration for Michelangelo (which he spoke in front of all the academicians of Florence) counted up the master's works in bronze and also mentioned 'una vergine Maria col Bambino in collo maravigliosissima, mandata in Fiandra da alcuni mercatanti de' Mascheroni'. This Madonna and the Child with his arms round her neck reminds us of some later sketches by Michelangelo (e.g. the one for Antonio Mini in the British Museum).
[6] Alexander Mouscron had warehouses in Florence and Rome. He dealt in English clothing materials.
[7] A fee of 100 ducats would have been rather little for an almost life-size marble group. Michelangelo received 450 ducats for the Pietà ordered in 1498 by Cardinal de la Groslaye, and 400 for his David in 1502, which did not include the cost of the marble. A few years later, when Michelangelo was working on the Sistine ceiling frescoes, living very economically and having no travelling expenses, he mentioned in a letter to his father that he was spending 20 ducats a month.
[8] In Rembrandt's atelier there was a cast of the Child Jesus of the Bruges group (in the inventory of 1656 it figures as 'a child, by Michelangelo'). This cast of Rembrandt's is reproduced in a painting by Jan Lievens (Hans Schneider, *Lievens*, Haarlem 1932, Plate 14; Louvre, No. 129).
[9] Heath Wilson, Ricci and Carl Justi maintain that the picture is painted in oil, but technically this is incorrect. We have here the usual Italian mixed technique of the period, with powerful outline drawing on a plaster ground, a thin layer of green earth, in covering resin, and a graduated heightening in white with tempera; the over-painting is done with transparent resin, except in the flesh parts, which are painted in pure tempera. Intermediate varnish and final varnish (vernice liquida) were also used.
[10] The painting and frame were not brought together again until 1905 (Poggi, *Kunstchronik* XVIII, p. 299 f., and E. Bock, *Florentinische und Venezianische Bilderrahmen*, Munich, 1902, p. 78). The frame bears the arms of Angelo Doni and Maddalena Strozzi. It is supposed that the painting was commissioned on the occasion of their wedding, about 1503-4.

[11] When the auctioneer Claridge of Curzon Street, London, exhibited the relief (not for sale) in 1829, he stated in his advertisement that the sculpture was 'bearing the date 1504'. This date, perhaps written on the back, has now disappeared. (W. T. Whitley, *Art in England 1821-37*, p. 202.)

November 1506 he joined the Pope in Bologna and began work on the large bronze portrait (since lost). The St Matthew thus remained unfinished.[12] It was kept in the Opera del Duomo until 1834, when it was removed to the Accademia in Florence. Wölfflin and Justi think that most of the work on the statue was done about 1504; Thode and Mackowsky, about 1506. Ollendorf has drawn attention to a certain influence of the Laocoön, which was discovered in 1506, especially in the expression and poise of the head. Grünwald has established that the antique 'Pasquino' was used as a model.

THE CEILING FRESCOES IN THE SISTINE CHAPEL. Plates 37-116. The ceiling painting, as reproduced in Plate 38, measures 45 × 128 ft.

Fresco-painting (fresco buono) is painting on damp lime wash. In this process the lime serves to bind together the pigments and also to provide the white colouring. Only a limited number of colours can be used and these become lighter when dry. The painter applies as much of the wash as will serve for one day's work; if the wash were allowed to stand for more than a day, a film of lime would be formed on which the painting would appear patchy. In Michelangelo's frescoes the edges of each application can be clearly discerned and we can thus determine how much he painted every day. In his time the ground was composed of two parts marble sand to one part mortar. To this ground of sand and lime, which was dampened the night before, and applied in several layers, was added a damp covering of marble dust and lime. The previously prepared drawing, or cartoon, was cut into pieces, each of which represented a day's work. The section of the drawing was then fastened on to the fresco ground and the outlines were traced with an iron stylus. (These traced contours, which were not always followed exactly in the execution of the painting, can be clearly discerned in some of our reproductions, e.g. Plate 50.) The fresco took about six weeks to dry. After drying, the ceiling paintings of the Sistine Chapel were partly gone over in ultramarine and gold. The colouring does not greatly differ from that of the 'Doni Madonna', but in the course of the four years' work Michelangelo tended more and more towards the use of subdued grey, grisaille-like tones. The modelling, especially that of the flesh parts, is lead-grey; the high lights have the full strength of the white lime. Grey, grey-violet, grey-brown, grey-green, olive-green, yellow, cerise, orange-red and pure black are used; the colours achieve their strongest effects in the shadows, in the half light they are broken with grey and in the full light with yellow.

The project of painting the ceiling of the Sistine Chapel was conceived by Pope Julius II in 1506. The contract with Michelangelo was concluded on 10 May 1508.

Scaffolding was erected a month later and on 27 July the ceiling was covered with lime as a ground for the frescoes. Numerous assistants took part in the work, among them Francesco Granacci, but they seem to have carried out only labourer's work. Giuliano da Sangallo gave Michelangelo technical advice, especially as to the means of avoiding 'efflorescence' – the formation of mould on damp masonry. Before Michelangelo began his work, the face of the vaulting of the chapel was painted to form a blue sky with gold stars. According to the original plan, the central portion was to be filled with grotesques and the twelve Apostles were to be painted between the empty spandrels.[13] Gradually the plan was extended until it became the final version, including the spandrels and lunettes, with Prophets and Sibyls instead of the Apostles; three hundred figures were executed, as against the twelve of the first project. Between the autumn of 1508 and September 1510 the eastern half of the ceiling was completed. This is the part beginning at the entrance and running from Noah's Drunkenness to the Creation of Eve, with the nude figures of youths, Prophets and Sibyls as far as Ezekiel and the Cumaean Sibyl. Between January and August 1511 the western half of the ceiling was painted.[14] On 14 August 1511 the ceiling frescoes were unveiled and on 31 October 1512 the first Mass was celebrated in the finished chapel.

The impression produced on Michelangelo's contemporaries by these frescoes was enormous and it has been maintained through four centuries. Goethe wrote in 1786: 'No one who has not seen the Sistine Chapel can have a clear idea of what a human being can achieve. ... The master's inner security and strength, his greatness is beyond all description. ... At the moment I am so engrossed by Michelangelo that even Nature makes no appeal to me, for her vision is not so grandiose as his. If there were only some means of fixing such pictures in one's soul! But at least I shall bring with me all the engravings and drawings after his works that I can find.' In England the fame of Michelangelo had already been exalted in the Academy lectures given by Reynolds (1769–91) and Henry Fuseli (1801). Reynolds called his style 'the language of the gods', while Fuseli said: 'A beggar rose from his hand the patriarch of poverty; his women are moulds of generation; his infants teem with the man; his men are a race of giants.' Another painter, Benjamin Haydon, objected to this exaggeration (Encyclopædia Britannica, 7th edition, 1838): 'His women may be moulds of generation, but certainly not of love.' And he attacked vigorously Michelangelo's monumental style: 'When you see an outline like iron, that is the grand style. When hands are twisted, heads distorted, one leg up, the other so far removed from the body, that you may question if it will return, that is the grand style. ... Every figure of his looks as if he was insulted and

---

[12] In his life of Andrea Ferrucci da Fiesole, Vasari says: '*Andrea was employed by the wardens of Santa Maria del Fiore to make the statue of an Apostle, four ells high* [about 7 ft. 10 in.]. *This was at the time when Cardinal Giulio de' Medici was ruling in Florence. At the same time* [1512-15] *four similar figures were allotted to four different masters: one to Benedetto* [Rovezzano, 1512], *one to Jacopo Sansovino* [c. 1513], *a third to Baccio Bandinelli* [1514-15] *and a fourth to Michelangelo Buonarroti.*' The contract with Andrea Ferrucci for a statue of St Andrew the Apostle is extant, dated 13 October 1512. Was there a second contract with Michelangelo for an Apostle statue at about the same date? (Cf. *Vasari*, ed. Milanesi, 1879, vol. IV, pp. 478, 479 – note 2, and 532.)

[13] In a letter to Francesco Fattucci, dated January 1524, Michelangelo says: 'The first design included the twelve Apostles between the lunettes, and for the rest a certain arrangement of compartments filled with ornaments, such as is customary.'

[14] The Ancestors of Christ, in the lunettes and the spandrels above them (Plates 81-102), were painted after the finishing of the last Histories and the unveiling, i.e. between October 1511 and October 1512; the cartoons had been finished by the beginning of 1511.

The two destroyed lunette paintings. Engravings, after lost sixteenth-century drawings, by William Ottley

preparing to return a blow. If they sleep they seem as if they would kick; if they move when they are awake, they seem as if all their muscles are cracking.'

The general view of the ceiling (Plate 38) shows the whole of the paintings except for the lunettes, which extend downwards on the walls. The three triple central portions contain the actual narrative (Plates 39–47).[15] Stendhal already recognized that 'spiritually we must separate these compartments from everything that surrounds them and consider them as separate paintings'. They narrate the three origins of the world and mankind: the first Trinity, the origin of the World: the division of light from darkness, the creation of the stars, the separation of water from land and with the latter the creation of living creatures on land and in the waters (Plates 39–41). The second Trinity, the origin of mankind: the creation of man and woman, the Fall, the exodus of mankind from Eden to the land of men (Plates 42–44).[16] The third Trinity, the origin of Sin: the Flood, Noah's sacrifice and

his covenant with God, the drunkenness of Noah and the continuing of Sin (Plates 46, 45, 47).[17] This ends the narrative of the middle compartments – the tale of mankind living in sin and awaiting salvation. Round these nine pictures are the twenty youths bearing garlands, who with their vigorous movements emphasize the same idea as the captives on the tomb of Julius, namely the vain efforts of mankind while still unsaved (Plates 58–77). The chorus of seers, Prophets and Sibyls, likewise points to salvation (Plates 103–116). The four subjects in the triangular spaces at the corners deal with temporal salvation, the deliverance from earthly distress, the miraculous deliverances of Israel (Plates 54–57). The victory of a boy and the victory of women are represented, the victory of weakness over strength and of the grace of God over violence. We see the triumphs of David, Judith and Esther; but the most significant of these pictures is the fourth, the 'Brazen Serpent'. 'And as Moses lifted up the serpent in the wilderness, even so must the Son of man be lifted up: That whosoever believeth in him should not perish, but have eternal life' (Gospel according to St John, iii, 14, 15). This prediction of the Redeemer's coming has its sequence in the pictures of the Ancestors of Christ in the other spandrels and lunettes (Plates 81–102).

The first two lunettes, painted above the altar, were destroyed by Michelangelo himself, when he walled them up (1535) in order to paint the 'Last Judgement' on this wall.

The Sistine ceiling frescoes have of course suffered during the more than four hundred years of their existence. Already in 1547 they are mentioned as not in very good state in a letter from Paolo Giovio to Vasari. In about 1570 parts were restored, especially 'The Sacrifice of Noah'. Further restorations were carried out in 1625, 1712, 1903–5, and 1935–8.

THE TOMB OF POPE JULIUS. Plates 117–135 (170–174; 188–190; Plates VIII and IX). First contract and first design, March 1505; it was stipulated that there should be forty statues, delivery within five years, against payment of 10,000 ducats. In April Michelangelo went to the quarries at Carrara; in ~~September~~ December he returned to Rome and set up a workshop in Piazza San Pietro. 'If only my blocks of marble would arrive

---

[15] Plate 41 reproduces what Vasari calls 'The Dividing of the Waters from the Land' and Condivi 'The Creation of the Denizens of the Waters'. Konrad Lange (*Rep. f. Kunstwissenschaft* XLII, 1919, p. 1 f.) and Adolfo Venturi (*L'Arte* XXII, 1919, p. 85 f.) accept in a way Vasari's interpretation, but Erwin Panofsky (col. 41–4) supports Condivi's theory. – Lange and Venturi, however, call the fresco 'The Separation of Sky and Water' because there is no earth to be seen in it. The Bible describes thus the third day of the Creation: 'Let the waters that are under the heaven be gathered together into one place, and let the dry land appear.' Which means that at the beginning of the third day the earth was not yet visible, just as on the second day.

[16] In Plate 48 the right arm of God is stretched out creating Adam, while his left arm is round the shoulders of a young woman and his left hand rests on a child. According to an ingenious explanation of J. P. Richter, the one figure is Eve, as she appears before her creation in God's mind, the other figure is the Christ child (*Thode*, II, p. 323; *Tolnay*, II, p. 35).

[17] The sequence of the narrative is altered in the ceiling paintings because Michelangelo wanted to use the large central compartment for the 'Flood' with its numerous figures. – Condivi, and following him Vasari in the second edition of his work, calls the first compartment not 'Noah's Sacrifice', but the 'Sacrifice of Cain and Abel'. This sacrifice was the cause of Abel's murder, the first sin upon earth; and if we are to assume that Condivi was right, then the subjects for the third cycle were even more appropriately chosen and the sequence of the three pictures would be correct.

The theme of the Deluge was chosen by Savonarola for his Lenten sermon of 1494 on the Ark of Noah: 'Ecce ego abducam aquas super terram – behold, I, even I, do bring a flood of waters upon the earth'; in this sermon Savonarola foretold the divine wrath and the fall of Florence. Pico della Mirandola relates that he trembled in every limb and that his hair stood on end when he heard this stern warning; Michelangelo must have heard the sermon too, for he did not leave Florence until October of that year.

from Carrara!' he wrote to his father on 31 January 1506. 'In this matter I think I have the greatest ill-fortune. . . . A few days ago a vessel arrived which had been all but sunk owing to contrary winds, and when I had succeeded in unloading it there came a flood which swamped everything in such a way that I could not begin work.' The work thus began without the blessing of the stars and elements. Condivi called the story of its execution 'The Tragedy of the Tomb'. On 17 April 1506 Michelangelo fled from Rome, feeling that he was not properly appreciated by the Pope and that he had been grievously offended. From Florence he wrote on 2 May 1506 to Giuliano da Sangallo: 'If I had stayed in Rome any longer, it would have been indeed a question not of the Pope's tomb, but of my own. That was the reason of my sudden departure.' But a few days later Roselli wrote to Michelangelo that people in Rome were saying that Michelangelo was frightened by the idea of having to execute the frescoes in the Sistine Chapel and that this was the reason of his flight. In Florence Michelangelo may have resumed work on his battle cartoon; the tomb seems to have been forgotten. The Pope had important political plans; he was thinking of war and of reconquering for the Church her lost territories. On 23 August 1506 he left Rome and on 11 November he entered Bologna without encountering resistance. He at once summoned Michelangelo thither, in order that he might cast his statue in bronze for the reconquered city. Michelangelo went to Bologna 'with the rope round his neck', as he himself expressed it; but the tomb seems to have been forgotten again. From 1508 to 1512 Michelangelo worked in Rome on the frescoes for the ceiling of the Sistine Chapel. After finishing them, he wanted to resume work on the tomb, but no agreement could be reached. In October 1512 Michelangelo wrote to his father: 'I am still doing no work and am waiting for the Pope to tell me what to do.' On 21 February Julius II died and on 6 May a second contract was concluded with the executor of his will. Michelangelo undertook to complete the tomb in seven years and not to accept any other work in the meantime; he was to receive 1300 ducats in addition to the 3500 he had already had from Pope Julius. He submitted a revised design. Between 1513 and 1516 the *Moses* and the two *Captives* were executed (Plates 117–126). Michelangelo had a workshop at the Macello dei Corvi and employed Florentine stonemasons. In July 1516 a third contract was made and a modified design submitted, but there was a fresh interruption owing to work on the designs for the façade of San Lorenzo. The following years were spent in unproductive work and in journeys to Florence and the marble quarries of Carrara, Pietrasanta and Seravezza. It was not until 1519 that Michelangelo was free to work on his statue of Christ and on the 'Boboli captives' for the tomb of Julius (Plates 127–135). In 1520 the contract for the façade of San Lorenzo was definitely cancelled, but work on the Medici tombs was begun. In 1525, while working on the Libreria, he first had the idea of completing the Julius monument as a wall-tomb. But no decision was reached, although Michelangelo submitted a new design in October 1526. He went on working on the Medici tombs. The year 1529 was spent in work as an architect of fortifications. On 29 April 1532, after prolonged negotiations, a fourth contract was drawn up, but then came the execution of the *Last Judgement* and after its completion in 1542 the work on the tomb of Julius, which had long been in the hands of assistants, was entrusted entirely to Raffaello da Montelupo and Pietro Urbano. 'I wish I had learned in my youth to make matches,' wrote Michelangelo in this year, 'then I should not be in such a state of agitation. . . . I do not want to go on living under this burden. . . . Only death or the Pope can release me from it. I have wasted all my youth, chained to this tomb.' In the fifth contract (20 August 1542) everything was granted that Michelangelo had requested in his petition to Pope Paul III. 'Master Michelangelo Buonarroti,' begins this document, 'undertook a long time ago to execute a tomb for Pope Julius.' . . . 'Master Michelangelo,' it says later, 'shall be authorized to entrust three of the six statues destined for this tomb to a good and esteemed master . . . and the other three, among them the Moses, shall be by his own hand. But as Master Michelangelo has given the three statues named, which are already far advanced, namely the Madonna with the Child on her arm in a standing posture, and a Prophet and a Sibyl, both seated, to the Florentine Raffaello da Montelupo . . . there remain for him to complete with his own hand only the other three statues, namely the Moses and the two Captives, which are all three almost finished. But as the two Captives mentioned were begun when the work was planned on a far larger scale (a much larger number of statues had been contemplated, but by the contract of April 1532 the number was reduced), they are no longer suited to this project. . . . Wherefore Master Michelangelo began work on two other statues, which are to stand on either side of Moses, namely the Contemplative and the Active Life, which are fairly well advanced, so that they can easily be completed by other masters.' At that time Michelangelo had undertaken a work for Pope Paul III, the frescoes in 'his chapel', that is to say the Cappella Paolina, a work which, as he himself says, 'required a whole man free from care'. In February 1545 the monument was finally erected. 'It can now be seen in San Pietro in Vincoli,'[18] wrote Condivi in 1553, 'not, as in the first design, with four façades, but with *one* front, this being one of the smaller ones, not standing free, but against the wall. But although the work has been so patched up and reduced, it is still the worthiest monument to be found in Rome and perhaps in the whole world, on account of the three figures thereon which are by the master's own hand.' (Plates 188–190.)

The lower storey of the architecture is the work of Antonio del Pontasieve (1513–14; but some ornaments – see Plates VIII and IX – begun probably as early as 1506). The four herms are by Jacomo del Duca (who, about twenty years later, helped Michelangelo with the Porta Pia). The upper storey of the architecture is the work of Urbino (Francesco di Bernardino d'Amadore), whose assistant Giovanni de' Marchesi is probably responsible for the four ugly heads underneath the candelabra. The contract between Michelangelo and Urbino is dated 21 August 1541. The Pope's coat-of-arms is by Donato Benti (1543). The four figures on the upper storey are the work of two independent assistants (see caption of Plate 188). About the Sibyl and the Prophet by Montelupo we may believe what Vasari says: 'Raffaello da

---

[18] Instead of in St Peter's, as was originally planned.

CORRECTIONS:

p. 13, right column, 3rd line from below: *December* (not September);

p. 15, left column, line 30: *Falconet* (not Fauconnet);

p. 18, l.c., line 5: *painter* (not sculptor); last line: *Plate V* (not IV);

p. 19, The Last Judgement – the size should read: painted area 48 ft. high, 44 ft. wide.

p. 20, r.c., line 47: *Lorenzino* (not Lorenzo);

p. 206, note 5: *Raffaello* (not Raffaelle).

Montelupo fell ill while engaged upon the work, he could not devote his usual care and diligence to it, so that he lost in reputation and Michelangelo was dissatisfied.' The Madonna was begun by Sandro Fancelli (called Scherano da Settignano), but also finished by Montelupo. Urbino had perhaps a share in Boscoli's statue of the Pope; Burckhardt calls its design 'unforgivable'.

MOSES. Part of the tomb of Julius. Plate 117 (118–120). Marble, 100 in. high. According to Thode, it was begun in 1506, but Knapp maintains that a consignment of marble from Carrara of 24 June 1508[19] was intended for the Moses as well as for the two Captives now in the Louvre. Vasari, however, states explicitly: 'While Michelangelo was engaged on this work, the remaining blocks of marble destined for the tomb arrived from Carrara and were unloaded at the Ripa'; at that time the Pope had 'his head full of Bologna matters'; this must therefore have been in 1506. Between the beginning of this work and its completion came the execution of the figures of Prophets on the ceiling of the Sistine Chapel, Joel and Jeremiah. 'When Michelangelo had finished the Moses,' writes Vasari in 1568, 'there was no other work to be seen, whether ancient or modern, which could rival it.' He praises especially the painteresque treatment of the hair – 'one might almost believe that the chisel had become a brush'. Stendhal (1817) says: 'Those who have not seen this statue, cannot realize the full power of sculpture,' but he also mentions the 'profound disparagement' which had been the statue's lot and quotes the sculptor Fauconnet, who declared that the Moses was more like a galley-slave than a divinely inspired lawgiver, and the painter Fuseli, who discovered in it a resemblance to a satyr or a 'goat's face'. About this time Goethe laid great store by a bronze copy of the Moses. The costume is imitated from antique statues of barbarians (an attempt at historical accuracy), the horns represent rays of light. 'The rest is entirely in the antique style,' says Condivi.

THE HEROIC AND THE DYING CAPTIVES. Belonging to the Julius tomb. Plates 121–126. Marble, 7 ft. 1 in. and 7 ft. 6½ in. These two statues were not used for the tomb of Julius, because, as we learn from Michelangelo himself, they could not be fitted into the reduced design. In 1544, while the tomb was being erected, the master was lying ill in the palace of Roberto Strozzi. The latter, a cousin of Caterina de' Medici and a great-grandson of Lorenzo il Magnifico, was the owner of banking houses in Rome and Lyons and had influence at the French court. He conspired against Grand-Duke Cosimo de' Medici and shared with Michelangelo the ambition of restoring Florence to its republican freedom. In 1544 Michelangelo presented him with the two statues, and six years later Strozzi gave them to King Henri II of France, who in turn presented them to the Constable Anne de Montmorency for his castle of Écouen; in 1632

they belonged to Cardinal Richelieu; in 1794 they became state property and so passed to the Louvre. The Heroic Captive shows a deep crack, which goes across the face and down to the left shoulder (retouched in most reproductions). The antique prototypes of these Captives were not the statues of fettered barbarians, but the Hellenistic representations of Marsyas, which survived in mediaeval figures of St Sebastian. Ever since Condivi's time captious attempts have been made to discover the allegorical significance of the Captives; almost every possible suggestion has been made, down to the 'personification of the mass for the dead'. Condivi writes (in 1553): 'Between the niches there should have been herms, to which, on cube-shaped projections, other statues were bound like captives. These represented the liberal arts and in the same way painting, sculpture and architecture, each statue with its attributes, making them easily recognizable. This was intended to signify that all the noble arts had died at the same time as Pope Julius.' Oscar Ollendorf has interpreted the Captives in the platonic sense, Werner Weisbach as triumphal symbols. A political interpretation which has not found support, was given by Vasari: 'These Captives represent the provinces which the Pope subjugated and incorporated in the Papal State.' If we ignore all these conjectures, and also those of Justi, Thode, Brockhaus, Borinski and Laux, if we wish to see nothing except that which the works themselves reveal to our eyes, these Captives become easily comprehensible, eternally human symbols: captives of life, of dreams and of death, struggling against the bonds of fate and relentless nature, Titans who wrestle in vain or relapse into redeeming unconsciousness. In this sense these eternally vanquished beings become the counterparts of the temporal conquerors, the Victories.

THE FOUR UNFINISHED CAPTIVES. Intended for the tomb of Julius. Plates 127–135. Marble. Youthful Captive, 8 ft. 6¾ in; Atlas, 9 ft. 1½ in.; Bearded Captive, 8 ft. 8¼ in.; Awakening Captive, 9 ft. Inserted by Grand Duke Cosimo de' Medici, who received them from Michelangelo's nephew, into artificial stalactites in a grotto at the entrance to the Boboli gardens in Florence, whence they were later transferred to the Accademia. Mackowsky made a technical study of these four figures, for he believed them to be 'more suitable than any other work of the master's for deducing valuable conclusions as to Michelangelo's methods'. He declares that Michelangelo did not transfer a finished model to marble following the schematic method of point-setting, but that he hewed into the block from one side in the manner of relief. Justi arrived at the same conclusion, quoting the descriptions of Michelangelo's methods by Vasari and Cellini and referring to the five unfinished statues: the St Matthew and the four Captives from the Boboli gardens. Justi speaks of an 'extraction of the statue out of the block from the front. . . . Anyone who knew nothing of its genesis would think that the St Matthew was an unfinished relief. Here we have the front half of a figure, the parts seen in profile or frontally having been carried to different degrees of completion; the other, rear portion, is still hidden in the untouched, quadrilateral block. . . . But it was intended that this apparent half-relief should become a statue in the round.' Mackowsky speaks

---

[19] The accompanying letter of Michelangelo mentions 'the large statue', 'two statues' and the 'statue of His Holiness', in other words four figures hewn in the rough. Laux (*Juliusmonument*, 1943, p. 158) assumes a much later date for the Moses: after 1515 or even after 1519. See the contract of 1542 (here p. 14) where the Moses statue is called 'almost finished'. This means that parts of the statue were probably retouched in the time from 1542 to 1545.

of the tools used: 'Nowhere can we find traces of the auger;[20] the whole of the work was done with punch and claw-chisel. In consequence the surface shows parallel strokes which remind us of hatching in a drawing.' F. Baumgart, in *Bolletino d'arte*, XXVIII, 1934, pp. 353-5, compared the technique of the St Matthew with that of the 'Unfinished Captives' and pointed out that the block of Matthew was hewn into from the front (about 1506, Plate 36), while the block of the 'Awaking Giant' (about 1519, Plate 134) was begun to be sculped at one of the four upright edges, in such a way that *two* sides of the block were used for the figure. (On Michelangelo's technique compared with that of the Greek sculptors, see: *Vasari on Technique*, ed. Baldwin Brown, London, 1907, p. 193; Stanley Casson, *The Technique of Early Greek Sculpture*, Oxford, 1933, pp. 128, 186.) The sculptor Adolf von Hildebrand was the only critic who denied that the four unfinished Captives in Florence were the work of Michelangelo's own hand (in *Michelangelos spätere Plastik*, in *Gesammelte Aufsatze*, Strasbourg, 1916). Panofsky (in *Studies in Iconology*, New York, 1939, p. 218) thinks a date as late as 1532-4 possible for the execution of the 'Unfinished Captives'. If this is accepted, and also Laux's suggestion that the Moses was made after 1519, the chronology of the Tomb of Julius would have to be revised. Tolnay, too, dates the 'Unfinished Captives' after 1534, but Laux (*Juliusmonument*, p. 420, Note 59) has again pleaded for the earlier date, namely about 1519.

THE RISEN CHRIST. Plates 136-137. Marble, 6 ft. 10 in. high. Commissioned on 14 June 1514 by Metello Vari and two other Romans, in return for a fee of 200 ducats. A black vein was found in the marble, which disfigured the face, and Michelangelo had to begin again. This first version, since lost, was seen by Aldovrandi in 1556 in Vari's courtyard. Owing to this defect in the marble, work was interrupted in 1516; on 21 December 1518 the new block of marble from Carrara had not yet arrived. At that time Michelangelo wrote to Lionardo Sellaio in Rome: 'I am also being pressed by Signor Metello Vari concerning his statue, which is in Pisa[21] and should arrive by one of the first vessels. I have never answered him and shall not write to you again until I have begun the work; for I am dying of grief and against my will appear to myself as a swindler.' The barges conveying marble from Carrara had been held up in Pisa owing to the drying-up of the Arno. The second version of the Christ was created in Florence between the beginning of 1519 and April 1520. Michelangelo's assistant Pietro Urbano was sent to Rome to erect the statue in Santa Maria sopra Minerva and to finish it there. On 6 September 1520, Sebastiano del Piombo wrote in a letter to Michelangelo: 'I must tell you that Pietro Urbano has ruined everything that he has worked upon. Especially the toes of the right, completely visible foot, which he has hewn off entirely, also he has shortened the fingers of the hands, especially those of the right hand holding the Cross, so that Frizzi says that they look as if they had been made by a baker of cracknels. . . . Also one can see clearly what

he has been up to with the beard; my apprentice could have done it more cleverly. . . . Then, too, he has knocked one of the nostrils about – a little more, and only God himself could have put this nose right! Pietro thinks he is a great master – poor man, he will never learn what it means to make such figures – for the knees of this statue are worth more than the whole of Rome.' Federigo Frizzi subsequently repaired and completed the statue. Nevertheless, Michelangelo proposed to his customer Vari that he should make a new statue, that is to say a third version, for he would hardly have made a replica. But Vari, who had been waiting for this work for seven years, wanted no improvements: 'It shows the loftiness of your mind, that you wish to replace a work which could not be better by one that is better.' On 27 December 1521 the statue was unveiled; on 12 January Sebastiano del Piombo wrote to Michelangelo: 'The statue makes a very good impression. All the same, I have said and caused to be said, in all places where it seemed to me fitting, that the execution is not by your hand.'

A WINDOW OF THE MEDICI PALACE IN FLORENCE. Plate 138. In 1513 Giovanni de' Medici, a son of Lorenzo il Magnifico, became Pope (Leo X, died in 1521) and in 1523 Giulio de' Medici, a son of Giovanni who had been murdered in the Pazzi conspiracy of 1478 (Clement VII, died in 1534). Under these two Medici Popes Michelangelo received commissions for several works which were meant to do honour to the Medici family. These works were: the façade of San Lorenzo; the transformation of the loggia of the Medici palace; a small aedicula in Castel Sant'Angelo; the Biblioteca Laurenziana; and the Sepulchral Chapel of the Medici. On the designs for the Lorenzo façade Michelangelo worked from 1516 onwards; he also made a small terracotta model which has been lost; then he entrusted to Baccio d'Agnolo the task of making a wooden model after his designs, which however did not satisfy him (Plate VI–a);[22] and finally, from August to December 1517, he (with the help of Pietro Urbano) made another model which included wax sketches of the statues and probably also of the reliefs. This model has also been lost and all we possess now are a few drawings in red and black chalk by Michelangelo's hand. The contract for the Lorenzo façade was concluded on 19 January 1518 and cancelled on 10 March 1520, a few months before the inception of the Medici tombs.

While Michelangelo was working on his models for the Lorenzo façade, or perhaps after this plan had been abandoned and before the work on the Medici tombs began, Pope Leo X decided to transform the ground-floor loggia of the Medici palace into a hall. 'Michelangelo,' says Vasari, 'made a model for the kneeling windows (finestre inginocchiate) of the Medici palace . . . and directed the making of perforated copper jalousies (gelosie di rame straforato), executed by the goldsmith Piloto.' Piloto worked with Michelangelo in 1520-4, when he made the polyhedric ball with the cross for the

---

[20] The auger was used by Michelangelo in his early period, particularly in the 'Drunken Bacchus' and the 'Pietà of St Peter's' (see Plates 9 and 15).
[21] He means, of course, hewn in the rough.

[22] This model is identified by A. Schiavo with d'Agnolos work; but Tolnay (1951, p. 166) sees in it 'una riduzione del modello del contratto', which must mean a reduced version of Pietro Urbano's model, which he made in December 1517 under the eyes of Michelangelo and took to Rome to show it to the Pope.

dome of the Sacrestia Nuova, the Medici Chapel. Piloto's 'copper jalousies' were later replaced by iron grills; or else, they have perhaps never been on that window, as Vasari gives contradictory information in the Life of Giovanni da Udine: 'Cosimo il Vecchio had made on his palace a loggia for the citizens to meet. . . . This loggia was now closed, following a design by Michelangelo, and was made in the form of a chamber with *two kneeling windows with iron bars*, the first of the kind erected outside palaces (le prime di quella maniera fuora de' palazzi ferrate').

A SMALL CHAPEL IN CASTEL SANT'ANGELO.
Plate 139. This chapel, dedicated to Cosmas and Damian, the patron saints of the Medici, shows the Medici ring in the pediment, while inside there is the coat-of-arms of Pope Leo X (1513–21).

THE 'PERGAMO' OF SAN LORENZO. Plate 140.
This sacrarium was ordered by Pope Clement VII in order to store there the relics collected by Lorenzo de' Medici. Michelangelo made his first design for it in February 1526, but the work was not finished before the winter of 1532–3. It is erected over the main entrance to the church and faces the altar. Over the left pilaster appear the three Medici rings, while under the loggia – over the door of the church – there is the coat-of-arms of Clement VII, in the shape of a horse's skull, also designed by Michelangelo.

THE BIBLIOTECA LAURENZIANA. Plates 141–143;
Plates VI–b, VII, VIII–a and b. Commissioned by Pope Clement VII. Michelangelo made the first drawings for it in January 1524. In the same year the design for the carved ceiling was also made, but this was finished about ten years later by Battista del Tasso and Antonio Carota (see Plate VII–c). In 1559, when Ammanati finished (with Vasari's help) the staircase of the Laurenziana, Duke Cosimo I de' Medici asked him whether it were not possible to acquire Michelangelo's original design for the carved ceiling. The floor, which repeats the design of the ceiling, was made by Tribolo (together with Sante Buglioni and others), the carved benches by Battista del Cinque and Ciappino, probably also from sketches by Michelangelo (Plates VII–b, VIII–a, b).

THE FUNERARY CHAPEL FOR THE MEDICI FAMILY.
Plates 144–169. Commissioned by Cardinal Giulio de' Medici, afterwards Pope Clement VII. Originally, in 1520, planned as a free-standing edifice with four tombs, for Lorenzo il Magnifico, Giuliano the Elder, Giuliano Duke of Nemours (died 1516), son of Lorenzo il Magnifico, and Lorenzo Duke of Urbino (died 1529), grandson of Lorenzo il Magnifico; then as mural decoration with two sarcophagi on each wall; then with the addition of a double tomb for the two Medici Popes, Leo X and Clement VII; executed after 1524 in its final form, which underwent various modifications during the work. The figure of the Madonna (Plate 164), which had been projected from the first, was to have been placed on the papal tomb. The final solution was that the papal tomb and those for the Magnifici were omitted, and the project was limited to two separate tombs for the Dukes.

The Cupola of the Medici Chapel. The Lantern designed by Michelangelo, the ball and cross by the goldsmith Piloto (see Plate IV-a).

In March 1521 the construction of the chapel was begun and the cupola was in position by January 1524. The *Madonna* was begun in the same year and should have been ready by the winter of 1531–2, but was still unfinished in the autumn of 1534, when Michelangelo went to Rome to paint the *Last Judgement* in the Sistine Chapel. Of the four recumbent figures the first to be begun was the *Aurora* (Plate 153), the dates of execution being: *Aurora*, 1524–31; *Crepuscolo* (Plate 152), 1524–31; *Notte* (Plate 156), 1526–31; *Giorno* (Plate 157), 1526–34, unfinished; statue of *Lorenzo* (Plate 148), 1524–34; statue of *Giuliano* (Plate 149), 1526–34. In addition to these, four river-gods were planned, which were to have reclined by the sarcophagi; an over-lifesize model for one of these is now at the Accademia in Florence (Plates 166–167). Participation of assistants: Tribolo began the 'Earth' for the tomb of Lorenzo, but neither the model nor the abbozzo of the statue has been preserved; Montelupo carved, after Michelangelo's model, the *Damian* on the left of the Madonna, while Montorsoli, who also helped to finish the *Giuliano*, executed independently the *Cosmas* on the other side of the Madonna (Plates IV-c, d). The *Crouching Boy* (Plate 168) was, according to a hypothesis advanced by Popp, intended, together with three similar unexecuted pieces, to crown the entablature. Various attempts have been made to interpret the allegorical meaning of the monument: Borinski saw in it allusions to Dante; Steinmann, to a carnival song; Brockhaus, to Ambrosian hymns; all three of them thus suggest a literary derivation. Tolnay gives an elaborate explanation, according to which the whole chapel was a synthesized representation of the universe, divided into its three zones

– Hell, Earth and the Heavenly Spheres. Jacob Burckhardt's opinion of the chapel (1855) was: 'Architecture and sculpture are conceived together in such a way, as if the master had previously modelled both out of one and the same clay.' On the other hand the French sculptor Henri Regnault declared (1867): 'I made a pilgrimage to the Medici Chapel. What wonderful blocks of marble live and move there! Unfortunately they are in a bad setting. This architecture, which is attributed to Michelangelo, made me quite wild. It is common and without charm, and it reduces and destroys the figures. Those little mausoleums, those tiny pillars and windows which surround the divine figures of the Thinker and Giuliano, made me turn livid with rage.'

LORENZO AND GIULIANO DE' MEDICI. Belonging to the Medici tombs. Marble, 5 ft. 10 in. and 5 ft. 8 in. high. Plates 146–151. Vasari mentions the collaboration of Montorsoli in the execution of both statues; according to Steinmann, his participation was limited to the helmets, armour and other details. Michelangelo made no effort to achieve portrait-like fidelity in the statues of the two dukes; to the Florentines, who missed this lifelikeness and were puzzled by the purely idealistic conception, Michelangelo proudly answered that in a thousand years' time nobody would know what the two Medicis had really looked like. Lorenzo represents the vita contemplativa, Giuliano the vita activa, as already suggested by J. Richardson.

THE FOUR PHASES OF THE DAY. Belonging to the Medici tombs. Plates 146, 147.
Crepuscolo, length of the marble block, 6 ft. 4¾ in.; Plate 152.
Aurora, length of the marble block, 6 ft. 8 in.; Plate 153.
Notte, length of the marble block, 6 ft. 4¾ in.; Plate 156.
Giorno, length of the marble block, 6 ft. 8¾ in.; Plate 157.
(Details: Plates 154, 158–162.)
Stendhal (in *Histoire de la peinture en Italie*, 1817) says: 'The statues in San Lorenzo are partly unfinished. This deficiency is rather an advantage in view of Michelangelo's powerful style.' Stendhal was also the first to draw attention to the resemblances to the Vatican 'Torso'. 'In both the male figures,' he says while discussing the *Giorno* and the *Crepuscolo*, 'one finds striking reminiscences of the Vatican "Torso", but transformed by Michelangelo's genius.' Burckhardt writes: 'In these four statues the master has proclaimed his boldest ideas on the limits and aim of his art. . . . For his successors this was the straight road to ruin.' Vasari wrote: 'And what can I say of the Night, this statue which is not only a great and rare work of art, but is also unique? Who, in any period, has ever seen a statue, whether ancient or modern, of such a high degree of culture? One can well understand that it was this Night which completely obscured all those artists who for a time sought, not to surpass, but to equal Michelangelo.' Daniele da Volterra made copies of all the figures in the Medici Chapel, and Tintoretto and El Greco, among others, drew inspiration from them. Of the many models connected with the 'Phases of the Day' only three have a claim to be considered as genuine, a small wax sketch for the *Giorno* in the British Museum, and two larger terracottas for the *Notte* and *Aurora* in the Pietri Collection (Plates III–d and IV).

MADONNA AND CHILD. Belonging to the Medici tombs. Plate 164 (165). Marble, 7 ft. 5⅜ in. Burckhardt says of it: 'It is hardly more than hewn in the rough. . . . Owing to a fault in the marble or a slip on the part of the artist, the right arm did not turn out as it should have done and was therefore adjusted behind as we see it to-day. Probably this affected the rest of the statue, which for that reason was completed only schematically and inadequately.' But to this Carl Justi added: 'We live in an age of revision of all values, of a fundamental transformation of the world of culture: and thus it happens that the most criticized of Michelangelo's marble figures, which previously was almost ignored, is now the most praised, as the most powerful expression of his style.'

RIVER-GOD. Modelled in clay and oakum, over wood. 5 ft. 10 in. long. Plates 166–167. On 24 October 1525 Michelangelo wrote to Fattucci in Rome: 'The four rough-hewn statues[23] are not yet ready and there is still much work to do on them. The four others, representing rivers, have not yet been begun, as I have not yet got the marble blocks in my house, although they have arrived in Florence.' The four rivers were conceived as allegorical figures for the bases of the two sarcophagi in the Medici Chapel, but the work does not seem to have progressed further than two clay models for the sarcophagus of Lorenzo, of which only one, much damaged, has been preserved (which would probably have been placed beneath the Aurora). Plate 166 shows approximately the correct position.

THE CROUCHING BOY. According to Popp, intended for the Medici tombs. Plates 168–169. Marble, 22 in. high. Its authenticity is entirely unsupported and therefore doubtful.[24] Hewn out of a square block, with maximum utilization of the volume. This figure, conceived as a crowning of the entablature, reminds us with its economy of height of the figures on the gable-corners of antique temples. (I have included this sculpture among the authentic works because I believe that it was begun by Michelangelo himself, although probably continued by Tribolo. One could say what Sebastiano del Piombo said about the Minerva Christ: 'However, I am telling everybody that the execution is not by Michelangelo's hand.') The statue is not quite finished. L. Brown, an Englishman, bought the statue in 1787 from the Medici collection in Florence, and sold it to the Academy in St Petersburg; in 1851 it was transferred to the Hermitage.

CLAY MODEL FOR A 'VICTORY' GROUP. Plates 170, 171. 16½ in. high. It is often called 'Hercules and Cacus' or 'Samson slaying a Philistine', but according to Springer, Wilde and Laux (*Michelangelos Juliusmonument*, Berlin, 1943, pp. 54 and 411) it belongs, like the group in the Palazzo Vecchio (Plate 172), to the tomb of Julius and is a model for a group which was not executed. (But cf. E. Panofsky, *Studies in Iconology*, New York, 1939, pp. 231 f.) There is a copy in wax in the Victoria and Albert Museum, London.

---

[23] Presumably the Madonna, Lorenzo, Aurora and Crepuscolo.
[24] Since these words were first printed (1939) two critics have doubted the authenticity of the statue: Kriegbaum (1940), who with good reasons attributes the execution to Tribolo, and Wittkower (1944), who suggests Pierino da Vinci.

THE VICTORY. Probably intended for the tomb of Julius.[25] Plate 172 (173, 174). Marble, 8 ft. 7½ in. high. Knapp thinks the group was destined for the façade of San Lorenzo; Brinckmann, too, thinks that it was not intended for the tomb of Julius and sees in it an allegory of the platonic Eros; on the other hand, Schottmüller, Wilde and Panofsky, are against this theory. Justi gave it a political interpretation, as symbolizing the overthrowing of liberty in Florence;[26] he describes the group as 'probably the most puzzling work which Michelangelo has bequeathed to posterity'. Mackowsky suspects the collaboration of assistants on account of the 'exaggerated modelling' and dates it about the same time as the Apollo, which was executed after 1530, thus assigning it to the same period as Justi. A resemblance between the features of the vanquished figure and those of Michelangelo was noted by the older writers (Symonds, I, 89); by assuming that the young Cavalieri, Michelangelo's friend, was the model for the victor, it was easy to arrive at an erotic interpretation.[27] The group was left unfinished in Michelangelo's Florentine workshop. The head is now in parts polished, which may have been done by some assistant; the pupil is incised in the right eye, but not in the left, which is also probably due to the same assistant. After Michelangelo's death the statue was in the hands of Daniele da Volterra, who proposed to put it, together with other sculptures, on the Master's tomb. R. Wittkower (in *Burlington Magazine*, 1941, p. 133) suggested that the head of the Victor is the work of Vincenzo Danti; Tolnay called this 'a not very convincing opinion'.

APOLLO. Plates 175–177. Marble, 4 ft. 9½ in. high, including base. In 1527 the Medici were driven out for the second time, but the Emperor Charles V joined forces with Pope Clement VII and laid siege to Florence. (Michelangelo was then responsible for the fortifications.) The city fell after eleven months (on 12 August 1530) and Alessandro de' Medici, probably a natural son of Clement VII and husband of Margaret, later Duchess of Parma, the illegitimate daughter of Charles V, was installed as hereditary Duke. Vasari relates: 'After the capitulation of Florence, Baccio Valori, as the Pope's plenipotentiary, was ordered to arrest some of the most prominent party leaders among the burghers. The court sent to Michelangelo's house to seek him, but, foreseeing this, he had taken refuge in the house of a friend near-by.' The Pope ordered that he should be found and promised him immunity from punishment if he would resume work on the chapel of the Medici family. 'When Michelangelo felt himself thus reassured, he sought first to win the favour of Baccio Valori. He made for him from a block of

marble, three ells high [about five foot nine inches], a figure representing an Apollo, who is drawing an arrow from his quiver. This statue, which was not quite finished, now stands in the chamber of the Prince of Florence.' Popp describes the statue as a niche figure for the Magnifici tomb and does not believe that it is the statue intended for Valori. She calls it 'David', which is in accordance with the Inventory of 1553, when the statue was in the collection of Duke Cosimo I de' Medici. Vasari's statements as regards measurements, material and date, fit this statue. The bulge beneath the right foot should not be interpreted as the head of Goliath, but might very well be the head of the python slain by Apollo, or just a stone.

THE LAST JUDGEMENT. Plate 178 (179–187). The largest fresco painting in Rome, 48 ft. wide and 44 ft. high. Frescoes by Perugino and two lunette paintings by Michelangelo were removed to make way for it. The windows in the altar wall were blocked up with bricks[28] and an inner wall of dried bricks was erected; between the wall of the chapel and this inner wall a space for ventilation was left. The wall for the fresco was built sloping, in such a way that it overhung at the top by about half a Florentine 'braccia' (about a foot), thus preventing the accumulation of dust. The ground for oil painting (mortar mixed with resin), which had been applied by Sebastiano del Piombo, was removed by Michelangelo, who painted in fresco on a ground of damp lime and mortar. He executed the whole work personally, being assisted only by an ordinary colour-grinder. He began the work in April 1536, the upper portion being finished by 15 December 1540, and the complete painting was unveiled on 31 October 1541 (twenty-nine years after the unveiling of the ceiling paintings). We are told that Pope Paul III, overcome by the sight, broke into prayer with the words:'Lord, charge me not with my sins when Thou shalt come on the Day of Judgement.' The fresco is arranged in three zones. The top one is the Kingdom of Heaven, with Christ as Judge of the World enthroned in the centre and the Virgin next to him; around him is an inner circle of Apostles in the right half of the arch, and Patriarchs in the left. Two Martyrs finish off the lower end of this circle. Above, in the lunettes, we see hosts of angels, with the instruments of Christ's Passion, the Cross, and the pillar at which he was scourged. In the other circle we have Prophets, Confessors and Martyrs on the right, and the Hebrew women, holy virgins and Sibyls on the left. – The middle zone is the realm of those who have been judged: on the left the ascent of the elect, on the right the fall of the damned, while in the centre the messengers of the Lord blow their trumpets. – The lowest zone is the realm of Charon and the demons; the Resurrection of the Dead and the arrival in Hell fill the portion immediately above the altar. – Justi described the 'Last Judgement' as 'Michelangelo's last word in formative art'. Weisbach saw in it the perfection of the 'heroic' style, while Dvořak recognized it as the 'source of a new style', and wrote: 'From the time of

---

[25] On this point see the detailed exposition by Karl August Laux, *Michelangelos Juliusmonument*, Berlin 1943, p. 46 f. Laux disagrees with Johannes Wilde (see Note 18, p. 411) and dates both Victory groups (our Plates 170 and 172) about 1525.

[26] Justi is here referring to the siege and capture of Florence by the Medici in 1530, when Michelangelo was in charge of the defence works (not to the victory of the Medici in 1512).

[27] There is a late echo of this Victory group in the 'Apotheosis of Prince Eugen' by Balthasar Permoser, 1721, in which the 'Vanquished' is actually an authentic self-portrait of the artist (reproduced by Ludwig Goldscheider in *500 Self-portraits*, 1936, Plate 295). If we wish to connect the 'Victory' with Tommaso de' Cavalieri, that would involve a later dating, for Michelangelo did not make the acquaintance of this good-looking young man until the end of 1532. Justi dated the group 1533–4.

[28] The preparations for the fresco lasted a year, from the spring of 1535 to the spring of 1536 (*Steinmann*, II, p. 766 f.).

the "Last Judgement" the whole of Italian art becomes michelangelesque, not only in its various forms, but in its entire trend of thought, which is filled with a new conception of ideal timelessness, of spatial universality, and with a hitherto unknown spiritual pathos. When we say that Michelangelo became the destiny of Italian art, this is true of none of his works so much as of the "Last Judgement", and if we wished to give an exhaustive study of its influence we should have to enumerate all the works produced in Italy, and in part to the north of the Alps as well, from its creation down to the end of Baroque art.' In contrast to the enormous impression which it made on contemporary painters was the zealotic hostility of theologians and men of letters, who were filled with the spirit of the Counter-reformation. Two opinions have become popular and almost anecdotal, those of the papal master of ceremonies, Biagio da Cesena, and of Pietro Aretino. Biagio, who saw the upper portion of the fresco in 1540, called it a 'stufa d'ignudi', a bathing establishment. In 1537 Michelangelo wrote to Aretino: 'I regret that I cannot avail myself of your ideas, but the painting has already progressed too far. . . . As for your resolution not to come again to Rome, you should not break it for the sake of seeing my paintings. That would be indeed too much. Adieu.' Eight years later came Aretino's attack, in the form of a long 'open' letter. He compared his courtesans' dialogue 'Nanna' with Michelangelo's 'Last Judgement', and claimed that he had displayed more pudicity than Michelangelo; he accused the painter of being irreverent. 'Such things might be painted in a voluptuous bathroom, but not in the choir of the highest chapel. . . . Our souls are benefited little by art, but by piety.' Michelangelo is supposed to have inserted the portraits of both these critics in his 'Last Judgement', Aretino being represented as Bartholomew with the skin of the flayed martyr, which itself bears a self-portrait of Michelangelo (Plates 182, 184). According to Vasari, he caricatured Biagio in the figure of Minos, the supreme judge of hell (Plate 183); the ears resemble a donkey's; Biagio complained to the Pope, who answered him with true Florentine wit that to rescue him from hell was outside his province; if he had been in Purgatory, that would have been a different matter, but 'ibi nulla est redemptio'. Nevertheless Biagio's opinion finally prevailed, and in a sitting of the Council of Trent on 3 December 1563, the representation of unsuitable subjects in churches was forbidden. Under Popes Paul IV and Gregory XIII Michelangelo's fresco was in danger of being completely destroyed. Finally the nudities were painted over, firstly by Michelangelo's pupil Daniele da Volterra, who thereby won for himself the nickname of 'il brachettone' or the 'breeches-maker'. Further overpaintings were undertaken in 1625, 1712 and 1762. 'The state in which the gigantic work has come down to us is one of such mutilation that it is impossible to form an opinion as to its artistic qualities' (Thode). Copies by Marcello Venusti (1549, Museo Nazionale, Naples) and by Robert le Voyer (1570, Montpellier Museum), and a large engraving by Beatrizet (1562, in eleven parts) show the form of the painting before the alterations.

THE TOMB OF POPE JULIUS II. Finished in 1545. Plate 188. See the note on pp. 13-15. The six ornamental reliefs, and other details from the tomb, are reproduced here as Plates VIII and IX. (The squares measure 30 in.)

THE CONTEMPLATIVE AND THE ACTIVE LIFE (Rachel and Leah). Belonging to the tomb of Julius. Plates 189, 190. Marble, 6 ft. 7½ in. and 6 ft. 10 in. high. Mainly by Michelangelo's hand, but finished and polished by assistants. On 20 July 1542 Michelangelo proposed that these figures, which he had already begun, should be substituted for the Captives, as the latter no longer fitted the niches (see above, THE TOMB OF JULIUS, p. 14). According to Vasari, Michelangelo executed the statues in 'less than the span of a year'. Vasari also says that one of the figures is Leah, symbol of the active life, and the other Rachel, symbol of the contemplative life. Leah is not holding a mirror in her right hand, but a diadem, through which she has already drawn the tresses of her hair; in her left hand she has a laurel-wreath. Condivi does not mention Rachel and Leah, but calls the figures simply the Active and the Contemplative Life.[29] He adds: 'In this Michelangelo, always a zealous student of Dante, is following the latter, to whom in his Purgatorio the Countess Matilda appeared in a flowery meadow as the personification of the active life.'[30]

BRUTUS. Plate 191 (192). Marble, 29 in. high. On the pedestal is inscribed the distich: *Dum Bruti effigiem sculptor de marmore ducit, In mentem sceleris venit et abstinuit.* (While the sculptor was hewing the effigy of Brutus out of the marble, he came upon the spirit of crime and desisted.) According to tradition this inscription was composed by the Venetian humanist Pietro Bembo (1470–1547). Vasari maintains that the inspiration came from Donato Giannotti and that the work was commissioned by Cardinal Ridolfi. In his *Dialogues*, written in 1545, Giannotti makes Michelangelo speak of Brutus: 'He who slays a tyrant, does not kill a man, but a beast in human form. For since all tyrants are devoid of that love which all men must have for their neighbours, so too they are without human feelings and therefore no men, but beasts. That tyrants have no love for their neighbours, is evident, for otherwise they would not have taken that which belongs to others and they would not have become tyrants by using violence to others. I speak naturally of usurpers and not of hereditary princes, who govern their states by the will of the people.' Knapp remains faithful to the old political interpretation and sees in the bust a reference to the murder of Alessandro de' Medici by Lorenzo. According to Vasari, Michelangelo gave the bust of Brutus to Tiberio Calcagni, in order that he might finish it – 'he himself having only executed the features of the Brutus with fine strokes of the claw-chisel'. On this point Carl Justi wrote: 'The head of Brutus remained at the stage of a sketch; only the draperies were elaborated; this trite and insignificant work is neither by the

---

[29] Michelangelo himself, in his memorandum of 20 July 1542 to Pope Paul III, calls them the Contemplative and the Active Life, not Rachel and Leah. The Active and the Contemplative Life play a prominent part in the *Disputationes Camaldulenses* by Cristoforo Landino (1468). The protagonists of these conversations are Leone Battista Alberti, Lorenzo il Magnifico, his brother Giuliano de' Medici and others. These conversations circulated in manuscript form in Florence and must certainly have been known to Michelangelo.

[30] Dante, *Purgatorio*, XXVII, 94 f.; XXVIII, 37 f.; XXXIII, 118 f.

hand nor in the style of the master.' Grünwald has investigated Calcagni's share; the retouching concerns mainly the robe and the neck, but in addition to this the chin and mouth and a part of the hair have been gone over roughly with a flat chisel, an instrument which Michelangelo used only in his very early work. Attention has frequently been drawn to the resemblance to busts of Roman emperors, but this resemblance is due to the toga and the shape of the bust, which were Calcagni's work. Calcagni (1532–65) came to Michelangelo's studio first in 1556; at that time the bust was still unfinished.

THE CONVERSION OF ST PAUL and THE CRUCIFIXION OF ST PETER. Plates 193, 194 (195–199). Each fresco measures 20 ft. 6 in. by 21 ft. 8 in.

Finished by Michelangelo when he was seventy-five years old. Badly preserved, damaged by smoke, restored and over-painted 'to such an extent that the original character of the colouring has almost entirely vanished; the colours now produce a disagreeable, almost ugly effect' (Thode). Most over-paintings in the first fresco are, however, by Michelangelo himself. This painting, finished in 1545, was damaged by fire in the same year (see Michelangelo's letter to Luigi del Riccio; *Lettere*, ed. G. Milanesi, p. 513). Both frescoes were restored in 1933; the restorer's work shows mainly in the landscape. Plates 193 and 194 reproduce the frescoes before restoration, whereas all details, including the two in full colour, are taken of the paintings in the present state.

Lomazzo (in his *Idea del tempio della pittura*, Milan, 1590, p. 53) was the first critic who had any appreciation for these two frescoes. He explains that they show Michelangelo's third and greatest style (the first style being that of the Prophets and Sibyls, and the second that of the Last Judgement). The Paolina frescoes had no appeal for the writers of the eighteenth and nineteenth centuries (although Blake copied some of the figures), but in the last twenty years Neumeyer, Baumgart, Biagetti, D. Redig de Campos, and others, have established a revaluation of Michelangelo's last paintings.

THE PIAZZA OF THE CAPITOL IN ROME. Plates 200–203. Michelangelo's original plan is known from du Pérac's etching (Plate 200). The outside staircase of the Palazzo Senatorio was begun in 1546, and at the same time the façade of the building was partially altered; but in 1580 the new bell tower was erected and under Pope Clement VIII (1592–1605) the façade was completely rebuilt. The fountain in the centre of the double staircase was added in 1588. Michelangelo was therefore only responsible for the outside staircase of the central building. The Palazzo dei Conservatori was finished in 1568 by Prospero Boccapaduli and Tommaso de' Cavalieri according to the Master's designs, but Jacomo del Duca enlarged, at a later date, the central window and transformed it into a balcony. The Museo Capitolino (on our left when we are facing the Senatorial Palace) is an exact copy of the Palazzo dei Conservatori and was erected under Pope Innocent X (1644–55). The elliptical pavement in the Capitol Square (exactly the same pattern as appears in Michelangelo's design of 1546, Plate 200) was only finished in 1940.

The façade of the Palazzo Farnese in the eighteenth century. Engraving, 1765

PALAZZO FARNESE. Plates 204–208. Begun by Antonio da Sangallo the Younger, who died in 1546 and left the work unfinished. Michelangelo was appointed by Pope Paul III (Alessandro Farnese) to continue this work. He was responsible for the balcony and the large coat-of-arms, the windows of the upper storey, the cornice, and for the upper storey of the courtyard. The balustrade of the balcony was added by Antonio Cipolla in about 1860; earlier engravings show the central window without balustrade. It can, however, be proved that this shape was intended by Michelangelo himself; the reverse of a Farnese medal, representing the Farnese Palace, shows the central window in the shape of a balcony. This medal was coined in 1548. An engraving by N. Béatrizet, dated 1549, gives an identical view.[31] The two smaller coats-of-arms are later additions (as can be seen from the engraving reproduced here). After Michelangelo's death, Vignola and Giacomo della Porta finished the building in 1589.

IL GRAN NICCHIONE DEL BELVEDERE (the Large Niche of the Belvedere in the Vatican). Plate 209. The lower storey was designed by Bramante (begun 1503) and had a staircase with semi-circular steps, the inside concave, the outside convex. Pope Julius III (1550–5) commissioned Michelangelo to replace Bramante's staircase by another one with a double flight of stairs, similar to that of the Palazzo dei Senatori (Plate 203). It has come down to us in an adulterated form; the balustrade and the fountain with the mask were added about 1700, whereas the antique peacocks and the pine-cone were brought there in 1618.

Michelangelo conceived the idea of transforming the exedra into a large niche, which means that the two upper storeys were added according to his designs; but the work was finished in the time of Pius IV by Pirro Ligorio (1562), who was responsible for the super-structure and the colonnade.

THE FLORENTINE PIETÀ (Entombment). Plate 210 (211, 212). Marble 7 ft. 8 in. Mentioned by Vasari in his first edition and must thus have been begun before 1550. In the same year, the French traveller Blaise de Vigenère

---

[31] Both views probably represent the model, not the building.

saw Michelangelo working on it: 'I saw Michelangelo at work. He had passed his sixtieth year and although he was not very strong, yet in a quarter of an hour he caused more splinters to fall from a very hard block of marble than three young masons in three or four times as long. No one can believe it who has not seen it with his own eyes. And he attacked the work with such energy and fire that I thought it would fly into pieces. With one blow he brought down fragments three or four fingers in breadth, and so exactly at the point marked, that if only a little more marble had fallen, he would have risked spoiling the whole work.' From Condivi we learn that Michelangelo was still working on this group in 1553. In his second edition Vasari says: 'At this time (1556) Michelangelo worked on it almost every day as a pastime. At last he broke the stone, probably because it contained many flaws and was so hard that the chisel struck sparks from it; perhaps also because his criticism of his own work was so severe that nothing he did satisfied him. For this reason, to tell the truth, there are few finished works by him from his late period, when he had reached the highest maturity of his artistic power of creation. His finished sculptures all date from his early period.' Vasari tells us later that Michelangelo gave the broken Pietà to Francesco Bandini, who wanted to have it finished by Tiberio Calcagni, but the latter died in 1565. When one sees what he did, one can only say that his death was a good thing for the group. He is responsible for the highly polished and minutely chiselled Magdalen, which must have been very beautiful before; he was also responsible for the polishing of the trunk of the Christ and the sharp folds of the shroud. The additions are harmless: the left forearm of Christ from elbow to wrist; the hand of the Virgin on Christ's left breast and a piece beneath it; parts of Christ's right forearm. Vasari proposed that the Pietà should be placed on Michelangelo's tomb, as was the master's own intention, but this was not done. For a long time the group was left in the open air in a vineyard on Monte Cavallo, "nel giardino del Signore Cardinal Bandini". In 1664 it had already been transferred to Florence, first to San Lorenzo, and in 1722 it was placed behind the high altar of the cathedral. Finally, in 1933, it found its place in a chapel of the north choir.

THE PALESTRINA PIETÀ. Plate 213. 8 ft. 2½ in. high. Burckhardt mentions it in the first edition of his *Cicerone* (1855), but refrains from giving his opinion on it. Wölfflin (1898), in his book *Die klassische Kunst* refers to the 'abbozzo in the castle of Palestrina', but this Pietà was first published by A. Grenier (in *Gazette des Beaux-Arts*, 1907). Wallerstein, Thode, Mackowsky and Davies maintained that it is authentic. On the other hand Schottmüller writes: 'The group is certainly close to Michelangelo's conception in his late period, but it has not the quality of the works executed by his own hand.' Anny Popp attributed the group to an 'imitator of Michelangelo', Ulrich Middeldorf thought of Pierino da Vinci. A note in Cecconi's *History of Palestrina* (Thode, V, 282) may refer to Pietro (*not* Lorenzo) Bernini. The work is not free from later revision by other hands. The material is a marble-coloured limestone which occurs in the neighbourhood of Palestrina. In my opinion it was begun by Michelangelo and finished by another hand;

two stages of this later revision can be detected. The head, right arm and legs of the Christ seem to me to be entirely by Michelangelo.

THE RONDANINI PIETÀ. Plate 214 (215). Marble, 6 ft. 3⅝ in. high (the elliptical base is 2 ft. 2 in. wide and 1 ft. 11 in. deep). On 12 February 1564, six days before his death, Michelangelo worked all day long standing in front of this group, as we learn from a letter of Daniele da Volterra to Leonardo the nephew of the Master.
It is assumed that he began the group before the Florentine Pietà and then revised it again – perhaps ten years later. The legs of the Christ and the free right arm are relics of the first version. The Rondanini Pietà was left as a legacy to Michelangelo's servant Antonio del Franzese. It is not known when the Pietà was brought to the Palazzo Rondanini. Goethe, who lived opposite the Palazzo Rondanini in Rome from November 1786 to April 1788, does not mention the work, although he knew the Rondanini collection well and had a cast made of a mask of Medusa which belonged to it. In 1952 the sculpture was bought from Conte Sanseverino by the City of Milan for 135 million Lire (about $180,000) and placed in the Cappella Ducale of the Castello Sforzesco.

THE PORTA PIA IN ROME. Plate 216 (217). Commissioned by Pope Pius IV from Michelangelo in 1561. A number of assistants were employed; Jacomo del Duca, the most important amongst them, sculptured the mask on the keystone after Michelangelo's design, and also (with the help of Luca) the coat-of-arms.
In the time of Pius IX it was damaged by lightning and then replaced by a 'torretta' designed by Virginio Vespignani (1853). An engraving published in 1568 shows the Porta Pia finished with the top-piece in the centre being of a simple, triangular shape.

ST PETER'S IN ROME. Plates 218-223. The year 1546 was an important point in Michelangelo's life as an architect. In this year he began his work on the Palazzo Farnese, the re-planning of the Capitol square, and the work on a clay model of the cupola of St Peter's. On 1 January 1547 he was entrusted by Pope Paul III with the superintendence of the works of St Peter's, and so he became the successor of Bramante, Raphael, Giuliano and Antonio da Sangallo. On the whole Michelangelo returned to Bramante's plan and removed as much as possible of Sangallo's constructions. But he only completed the drum of the dome, and after his death Vignola, Giacomo della Porta and Domenico Fontana completed the dome after a large wooden model (Plate 223) which Giovanni Franzese had made from designs and under the eyes of the Master. This model measures one-fifteenth of the actual cupola, namely 17 ft. 8 in. high and 12 ft. 8 in. wide. Vasari says: 'The completion of the model caused great satisfaction not only to Michelangelo's friends but to all Rome.' But the baroque façade, which Carlo Maderna built for the church (1607-14), and Bernini's colonnades have deviated so much from Michelangelo's intentions that (as Knapp pointed out) one can only feel what Michelangelo contemplated if one looks at the back of the church from a great distance and sees the large dome against a clear sky. (Compare Plate X.)

THE PLATES

CORRECTIONS:

Plate 79: read *Joram* (instead of Jonah).

Plates 202 and 203: instead of the less usual 'Palazzo del Senatore', read *Palazzo Senatorio*, or *Palazzo dei Senatori*.

Plate 209: Nicchione *del* Belvedere is preferable (although Frey's well-known essay is entitled 'Nicchione di Belvedere').

1. MADONNA OF THE STAIRS. About 1491. Florence, Casa Buonarroti

2. BATTLE OF THE CENTAURS. About 1492. Florence, Casa Buonarroti

3. BATTLE OF THE CENTAURS. Detail of Plate 2

4–5. SAINT PROCULUS and SAINT PETRONIUS. 1494–1495. Bologna, San Domenico

6. ANGEL WITH CANDLESTICK. 1494–1495. Bologna, San Domenico

7. BACCHUS. 1496–1497. Florence,
Museo Nazionale del Bargello

8. SATYR. Figure at the
back of Bacchus, Plate 7

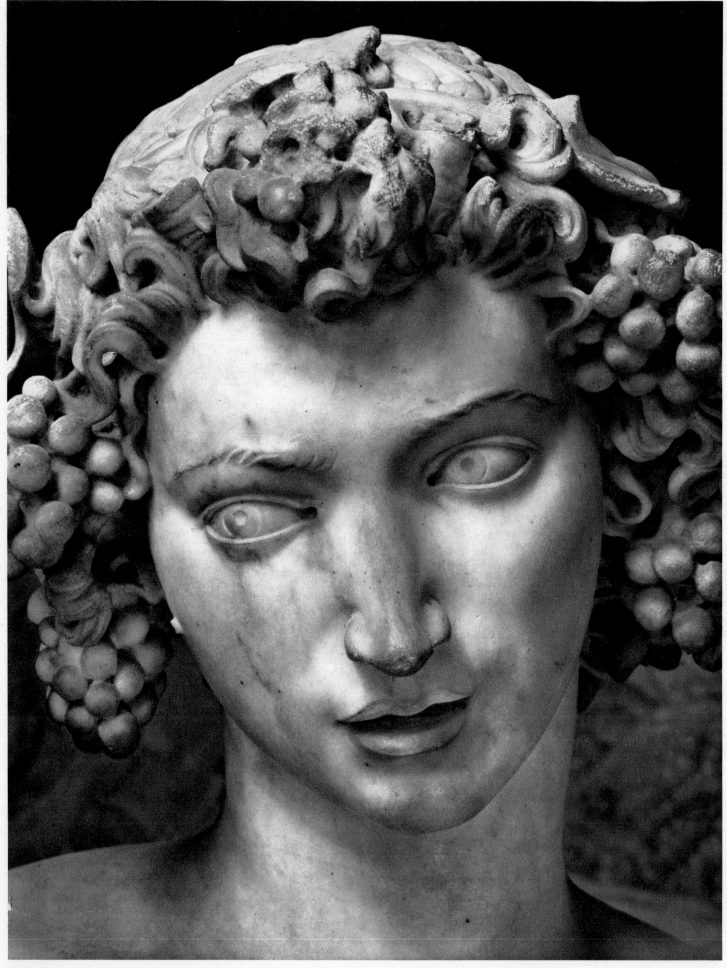

9. HEAD OF BACCHUS. Detail of Plate 7

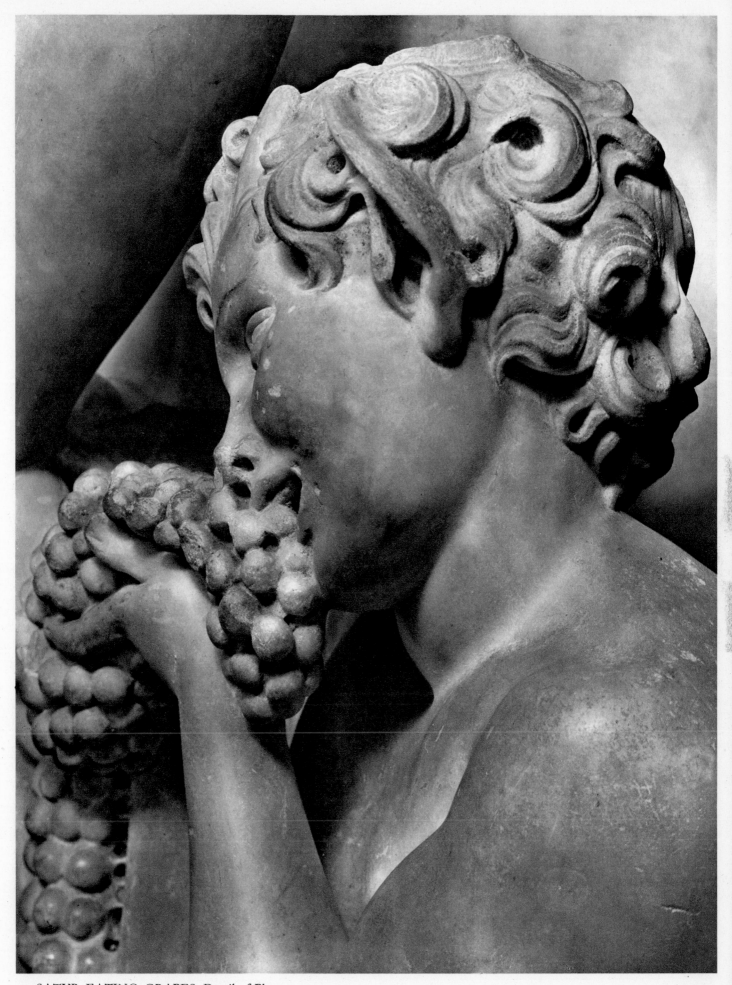

10. SATYR EATING GRAPES. Detail of Plate 7

11. PIETÀ. 1498–1499. Rome, St. Peter's

12. HEAD OF THE MADONNA. Detail of the Pietà, Plate 11

13. PIETÀ. Detail of Plate 11

14. THE LEGS OF CHRIST. Detail of the Pietà, Plate 11

15. HEAD OF CHRIST. Detail of the Pietà, Plate 11

16. HEAD OF THE MADONNA. Detail of the Pietà, Plate 11

17. DAVID. 1501–1504.
Florence, Accademia

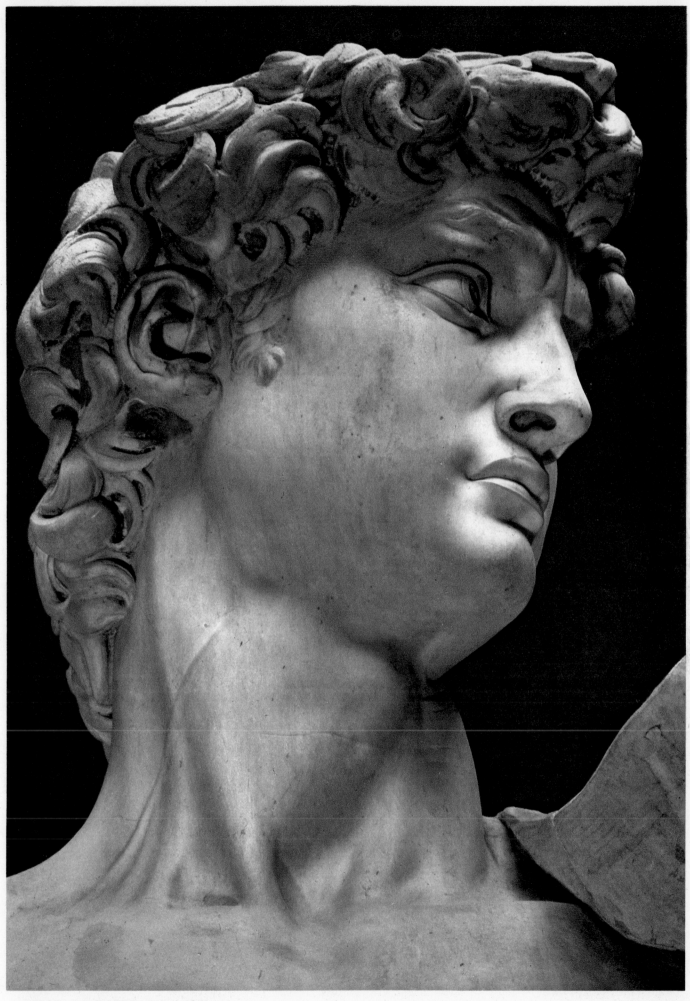

18. HEAD OF DAVID. Detail of Plate 17

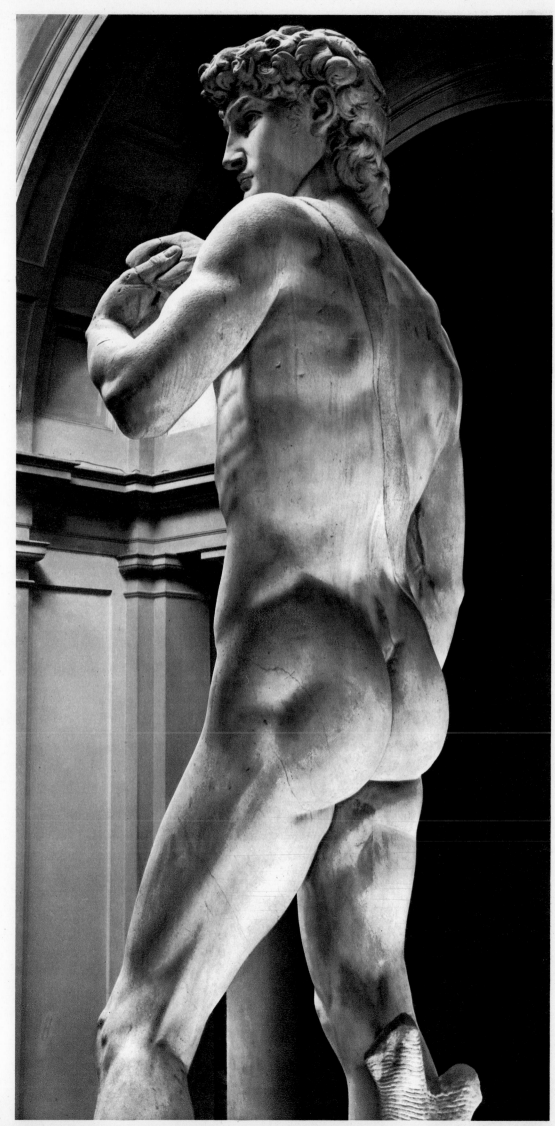

19-21. DAVID. 1501-1504.
Florence, Accademia

22. THE RIGHT HAND OF DAVID. Front view, detail of Plate 17

23. THE RIGHT HAND OF DAVID. Back view, detail of Plate 17

24-27. FOUR STATUES OF THE PICCOLOMINI ALTAR IN THE SIENA CATHEDRAL. 1501-1504

Pope Pius I—Gregory the Great—Saint Francis—Saint Peter

28. SAINT PAUL (two views). Piccolomini Altar, Siena Cathedral. 1501–1504

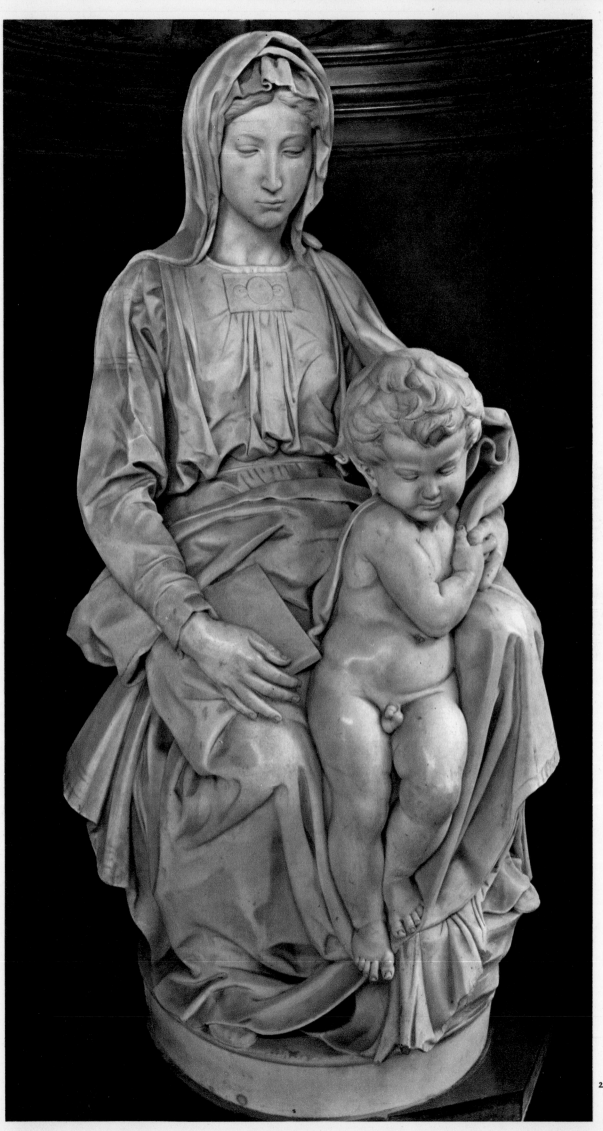

29. MADONNA AND
CHILD. About 1504.
Bruges, Notre-Dame

HEAD OF THE MADONNA OF BRUGES. Detail of Plate 29

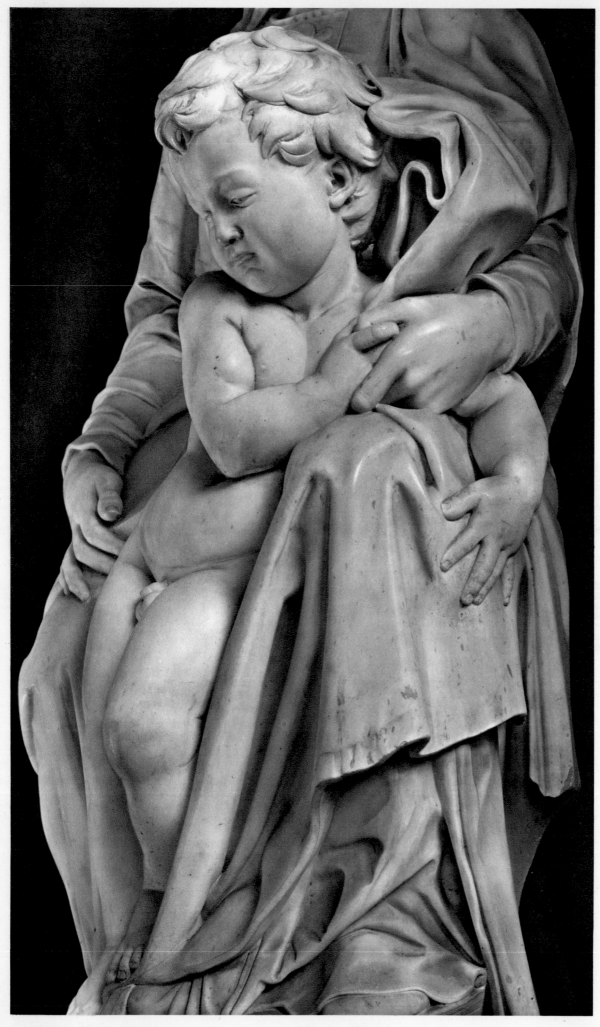

31. THE INFANT JESUS. Detail of the Madonna of Bruges, Plate 29

32. HEAD OF THE INFANT JESUS. Detail of the Madonna of Bruges, Plate 29

33. MADONNA PITTI. About 1504. Florence, Museo Nazionale del Bargello

34. THE HOLY FAMILY. About 1504. Florence, Uffizi

35. MADONNA TADDEI. About 1505. London, Royal Academy

36. SAINT MATTHEW.
About 1505–1506.
Florence, Accademia

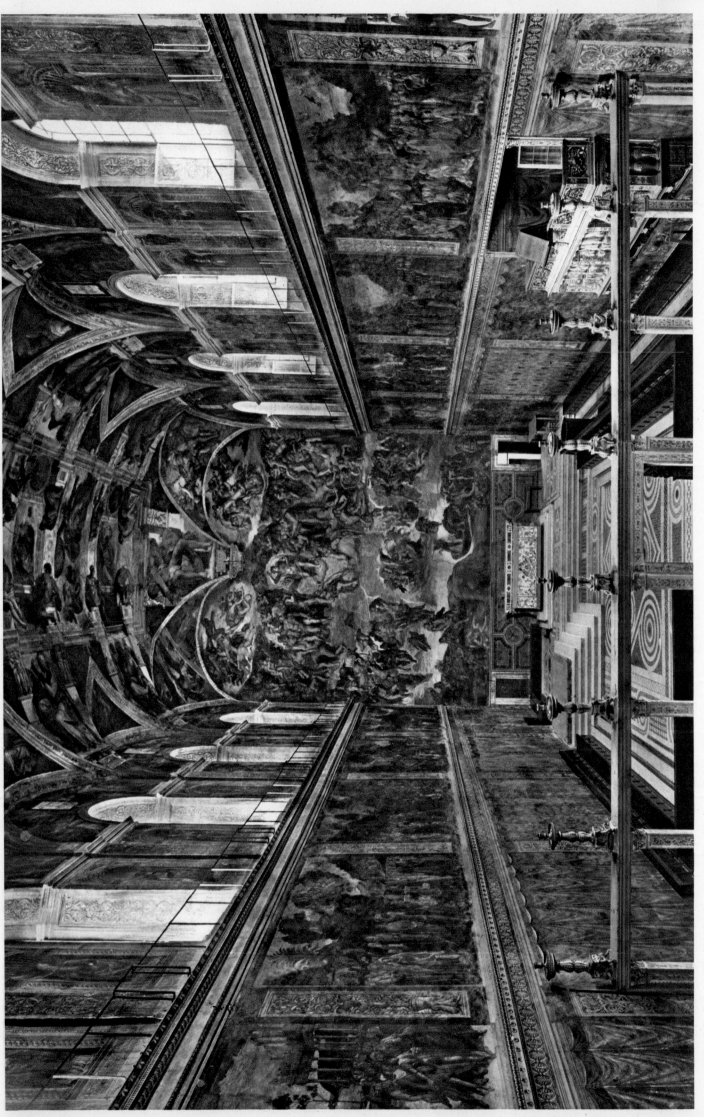

37. INTERIOR OF THE SISTINE CHAPEL, Vatican Palace, Rome

9. GOD DIVIDING THE LIGHT FROM THE DARKNESS. 1511. Section of the Sistine Chapel Ceiling

40. CREATION OF SUN AND MOON, AND CREATION OF THE PLANTS. 1511. Section of the Sistine Chapel Ceiling

41. GOD DIVIDING THE WATERS FROM THE EARTH. 1511. Section of the Sistine Chapel Ceiling

42. CREATION OF MAN. 1511. Section of the Sistine Chapel Ceiling

44. THE FALL OF MAN AND THE EXPULSION FROM THE GARDEN OF EDEN. 1509–1510. Section of the Sistine Chapel Ceiling

46. THE GREAT FLOOD. 1508–1509. Section of the Sistine Chapel Ceiling

47. THE DRUNKENNESS OF NOAH. 1508-1509. Section of the Sistine Chapel Ceiling

50. HEAD OF ADAM. Detail of the Creation of Man, Plate 42

51. IMAGE OF EVE. Detail of the Creation of Man, Plate 42

52. HEAD OF JEHOVAH. Detail of the Creation of Sun and Moon, Plate 40

53. HEAD AND RIGHT ARM OF JEHOVAH. Detail of God dividing the Waters from the Earth, Plate 41

54

55

THE MIRACULOUS SALVATIONS OF ISRAEL. Corner-spandrels of the Sistine Chapel Ceiling, 1509
54. David's Victory over Goliath.   55. Judith and Holofernes

56

57

THE MIRACULOUS SALVATIONS OF ISRAEL. Corner-spandrels of the Sistine Chapel Ceiling, 1511
56. The brazen Serpent.   57. Esther and Haman

58. NUDE YOUTH. 1510. Sistine Chapel Ceiling

9. NUDE YOUTH. 1510. Sistine Chapel Ceiling

60. NUDE YOUTH. 1510. Sistine Chapel Ceiling

61. NUDE YOUTH. 1510. Sistine Chapel Ceiling

62. NUDE YOUTH. 1510. Sistine Chapel Ceiling

3. NUDE YOUTH. 1510. Sistine Chapel Ceiling

64. NUDE YOUTH. 1510. Sistine Chapel Ceiling

65. NUDE YOUTH. 1510. Sistine Chapel Ceiling

66. NUDE YOUTH. 1510. Sistine Chapel Ceiling

57. NUDE YOUTH. 1509. Sistine Chapel Ceiling

68. NUDE YOUTH. 1509. Sistine Chapel Ceiling

69. NUDE YOUTH. 1509. Sistine Chapel Ceiling

70. NUDE YOUTH. 1508–1509. Sistine Chapel Ceiling

71. NUDE YOUTH. 1508-1509. Sistine Chapel Ceiling

72. NUDE YOUTH. 1508–1509. Sistine Chapel Ceiling

3. NUDE YOUTH. 1508–1509. Sistine Chapel Ceiling

74. NUDE YOUTH. 1508–1509. Sistine Chapel Ceiling

75. NUDE YOUTH. 1508–1509. Sistine Chapel Ceiling

76. NUDE YOUTH. 1508–1509. Sistine Chapel Ceiling

77. HEAD OF A YOUTH. 1508–1509. Sistine Chapel Ceiling
(The greater part of this figure was destroyed by a gunpowder explosion in the year 1797)

78. CORNER DECORATION above the Brazen Serpent spandrel: Bronze-coloured nude and grey putti. 1511. Sistine Chapel Ceiling

79–80. TWO OF THE BRONZE-COLOURED MEDALLIONS BETWEEN THE IGNUDI. 1510–12. Sistine Chapel Ceiling
(79) THE DEATH OF JONAH. (80) THE DESTRUCTION OF THE WORSHIPPERS OF BAAL

81–82. THE ANCESTORS OF CHRIST. Salmon, Roboam. 1511–1512. Spandrels of Sistine Chapel Ceiling

83-84. THE ANCESTORS OF CHRIST. Ozias, Zerobabel. 1511-1512. Spandrels of Sistine Chapel Ceiling

85–86. THE ANCESTORS OF CHRIST. Josias, Ezekias. 1511–1512. Spandrels of Sistine Chapel Ceiling

87–88. THE ANCESTORS OF CHRIST. Asa, Jesse. 1511–1512. Spandrels of Sistine Chapel Ceiling

89. THE ANCESTORS OF CHRIST. 1511–1512. A window in the Sistine Chapel, the lunette painted by Michelangelo

90-101. THE ANCESTORS OF CHRIST. 1511-1512. Lunettes in the Sistine Chapel

102. THE ANCESTORS OF CHRIST. 1511–1512. A window in the Sistine Chapel, the lunette painted by Michelangelo

103. ERYTHRAEAN SIBYL. 1509. Sistine Chapel Ceiling

04. DELPHIC SIBYL. 1509. Sistine Chapel Ceiling

105. PERSIAN SIBYL. 1511. Sistine Chapel Ceiling

PERSIAN SIBYL. Sistine Chapel Ceiling

CUMAEAN SIBYL. Sistine Chapel Ceiling

106. CUMAEAN SIBYL. 1510. Sistine Chapel Ceiling

107. LIBYAN SIBYL. 1511. Sistine Chapel Ceiling

108. HEAD OF THE LIBYAN SIBYL. Detail of Plate 107

109. JONAH. 1511. Sistine Chapel Ceiling

10. DANIEL. 1511. Sistine Chapel Ceiling

III. ISAIAH. 1509. Sistine Chapel Ceiling

112. JOEL. 1509. Sistine Chapel Ceiling

113. ZECHARIAH. 1509. Sistine Chapel Ceiling

ZECHARIAH. Sistine Chapel Ceiling

ISAIAH. Sistine Chapel Ceiling

114. EZEKIEL. 1509–1510. Sistine Chapel Ceiling

115. JEREMIAH. 1511. Sistine Chapel Ceiling

116. HEAD OF JEREMIAH. Detail of Plate 115

117. MOSES. 1513–1516. Rome, San Pietro in Vincoli

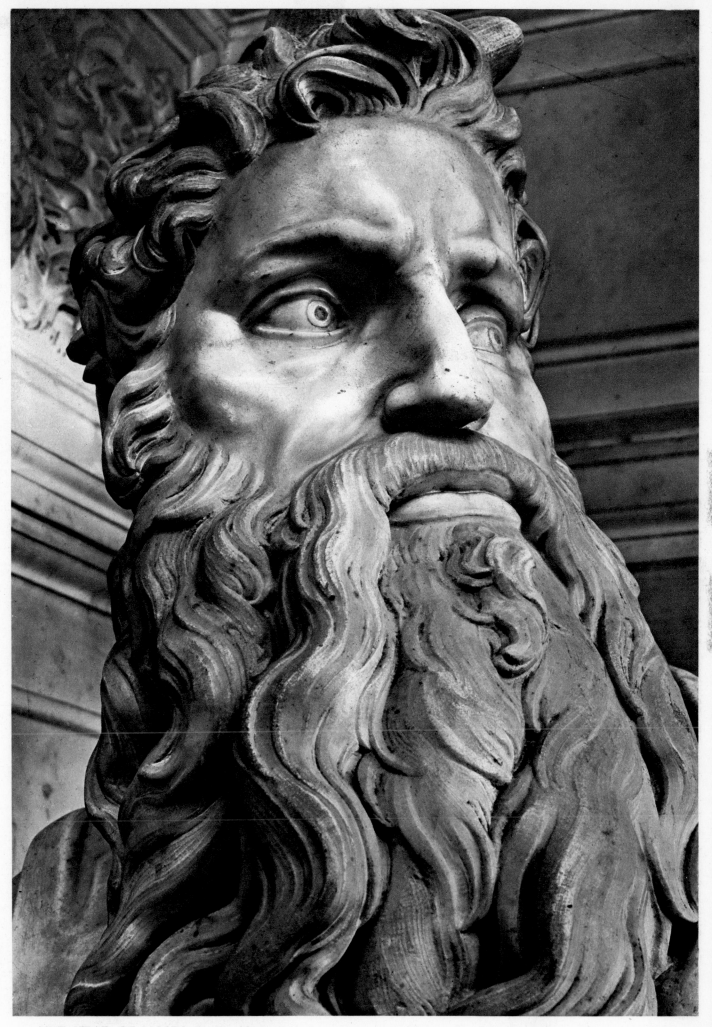

118. THE HEAD OF MOSES. Detail of Plate 117

119. THE RIGHT HAND OF MOSES. Detail of Plate 117

THE LEFT HAND OF MOSES. Detail of Plate 117

121–122. THE HEROIC CAPTIVE. 1514–1516. Paris, Louvre

123. HEAD OF THE HEROIC CAPTIVE. Detail of Plate 122

124-125. THE DYING CAPTIVE. 1514-1516. Paris, Louvre

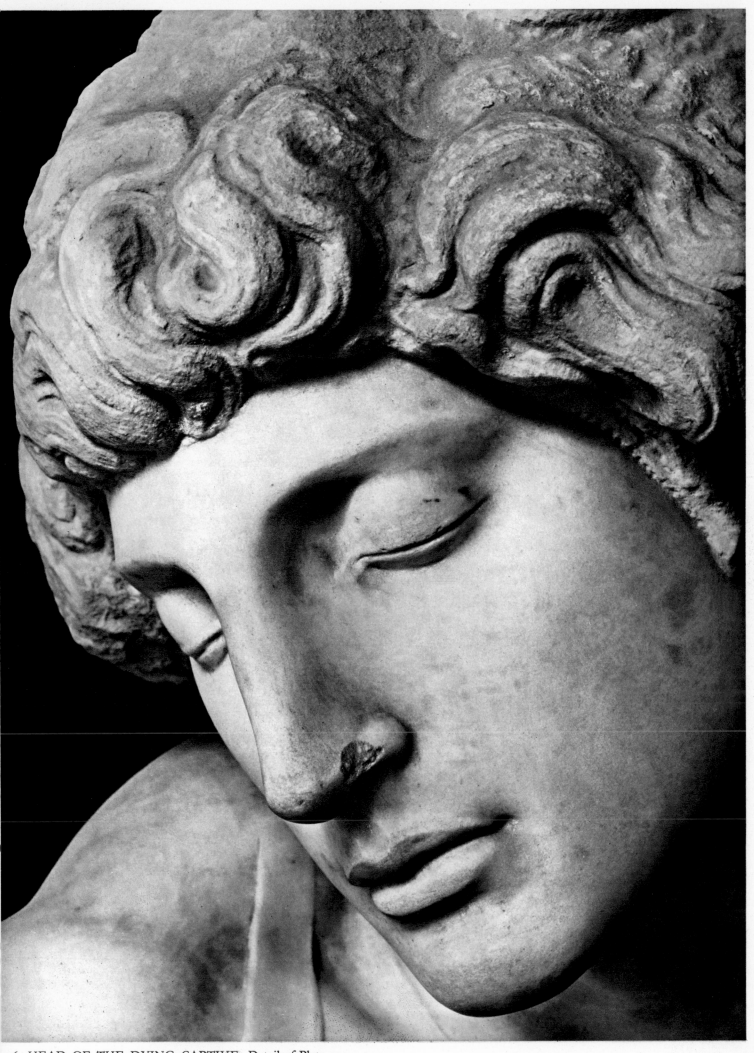

126. HEAD OF THE DYING CAPTIVE. Detail of Plate 125

127-128. CAPTIVE (I) FROM THE BOBOLI GARDENS. About 1519. Florence, Accademia. ("THE YOUNG GIANT")

129–130. CAPTIVE (II) FROM THE BOBOLI GARDENS. About 1519. Florence, Accademia. ("THE GIANT CALLED ATLAS")

131-132. CAPTIVE (III) FROM THE BOBOLI GARDENS. About 1519. Florence, Accademia. ("THE BEARDED GIANT")

HEAD OF THE BEARDED GIANT. Detail of Plate 131

134–135. CAPTIVE (IV) FROM THE BOBOLI GARDENS. About 1519. Florence, Accademia. ("THE AWAKING GIANT")

136–137. THE RISEN CHRIST. 1519–1520. Rome, Santa Maria sopra Minerva

138. WINDOW OF THE MEDICI PALACE, FLORENCE. About 1519–1520

139. FAÇADE OF A SMALL CHAPEL, Castel Sant' Angelo, Cortile delle Palle, Rome. About 1515–1522

140. THE "PERGAMO" OF SAN LORENZO, FLORENCE. About 1526–1533

141. THE VESTIBULE OF THE BIBLIOTECA LAURENZIANA. About 1524–1526

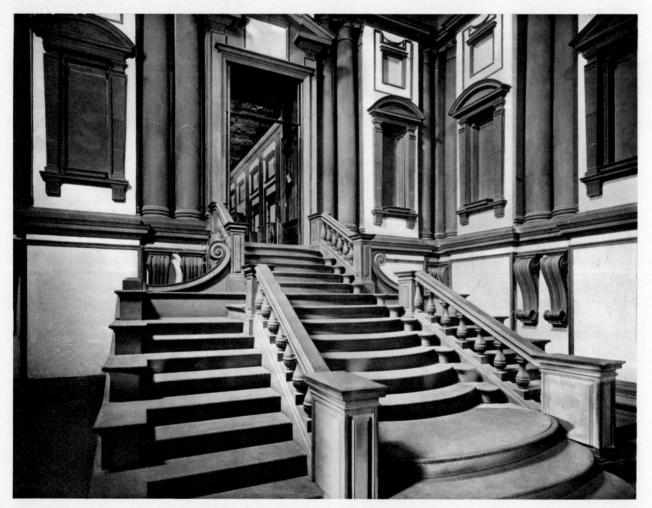

142. THE STAIRCASE OF THE BIBLIOTECA LAURENZIANA. Finished in 1559 by Ammanati and Vasari

3. THE VESTIBULE OF THE BIBLIOTECA LAURENZIANA. About 1524–1526

144–145. THE MEDICI CHAPEL. San Lorenzo, Sagrestia Nuova, Florence. 1520–1534

146. TOMB OF LORENZO
DE' MEDICI

147. TOMB OF GIULIANO
DE' MEDICI

148. LORENZO DE' MEDICI, Duke of Urbino. Detail of Plate 146. Florence, Medici Chapel

49. GIULIANO DE' MEDICI, Duke of Nemours. Detail of Plate 147. Florence, Medici Chapel

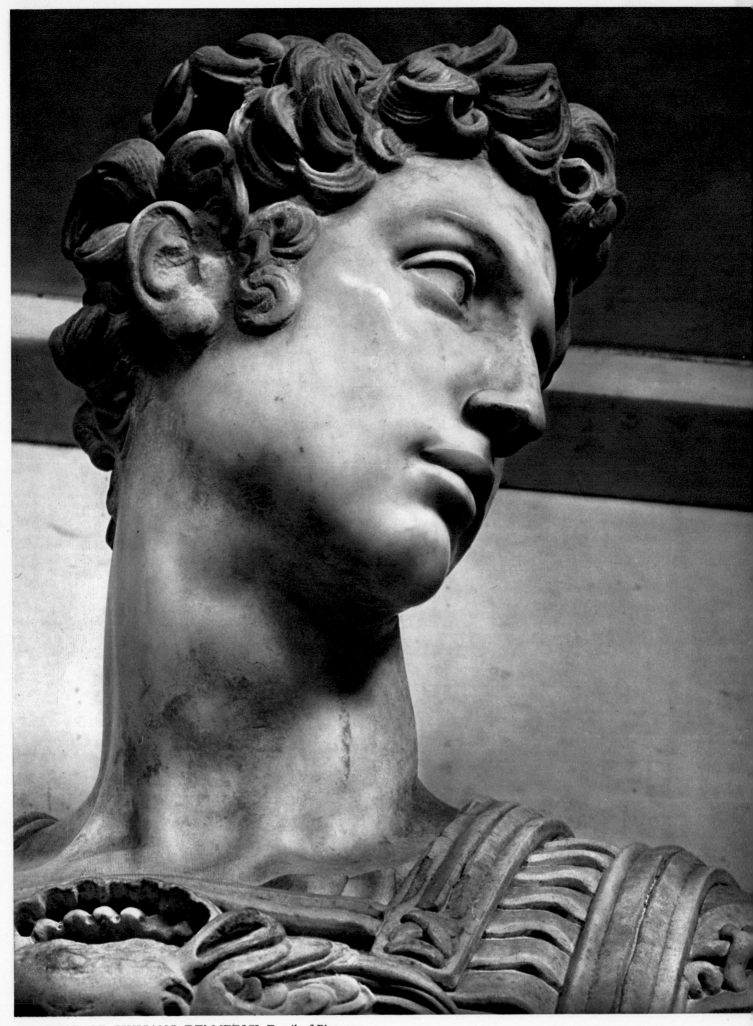

150. HEAD OF GIULIANO DE' MEDICI. Detail of Plate 149

151. HEAD OF LORENZO DE' MEDICI. Detail of Plate 148

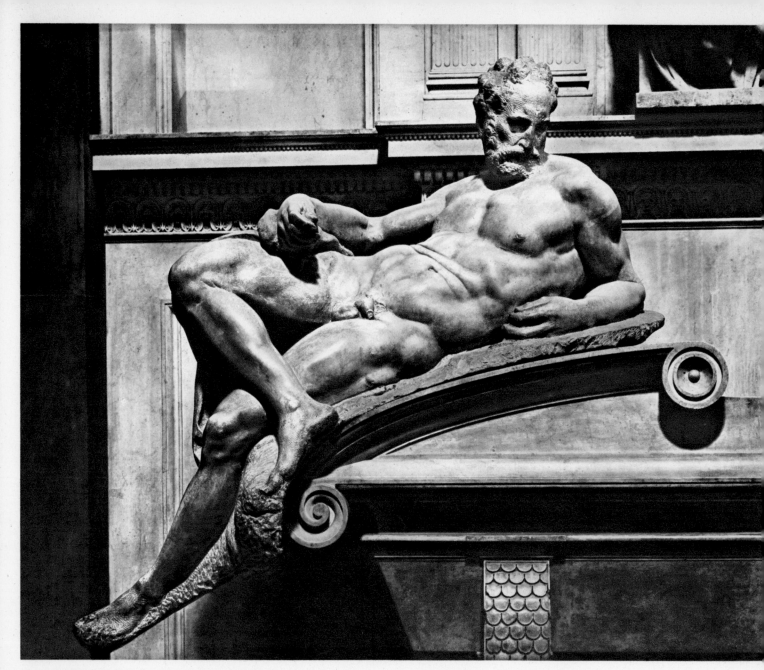

152. CREPUSCOLO (Evening). Detail of Plate 146

AURORA (Dawn). Detail of Plate 146

154. CREPUSCOLO. Detail of Plate 152

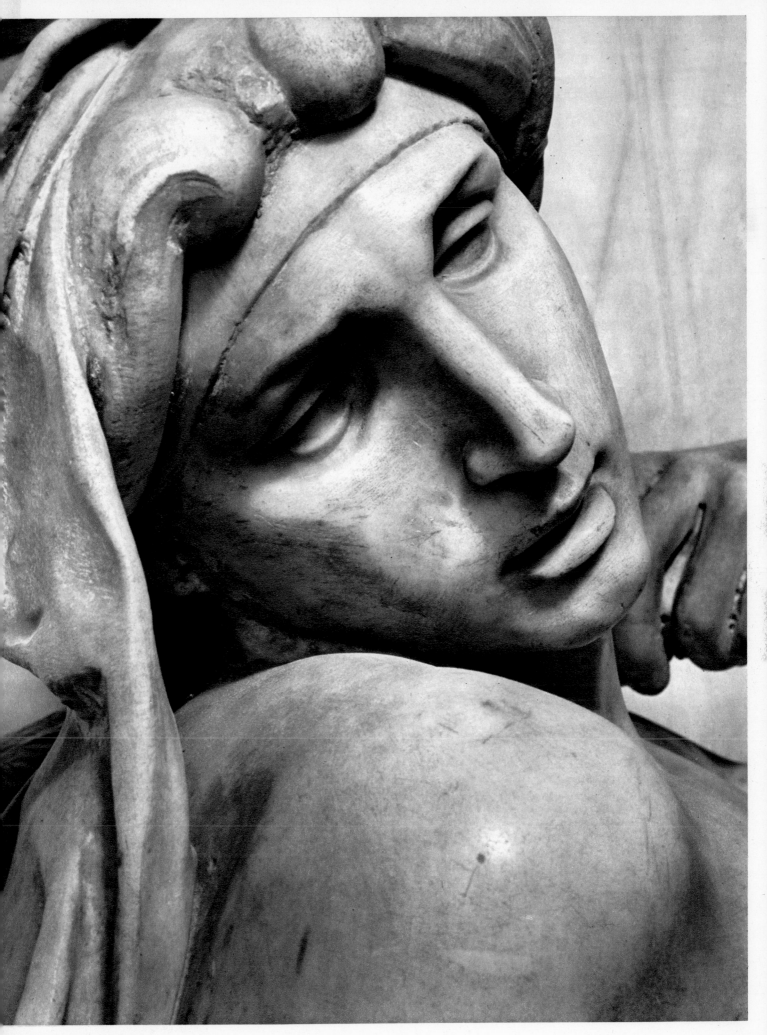

AURORA. Detail of Plate 153

156. NOTTE (Night). Detail of Plate 147

GIORNO (Day). Detail of Plate 147

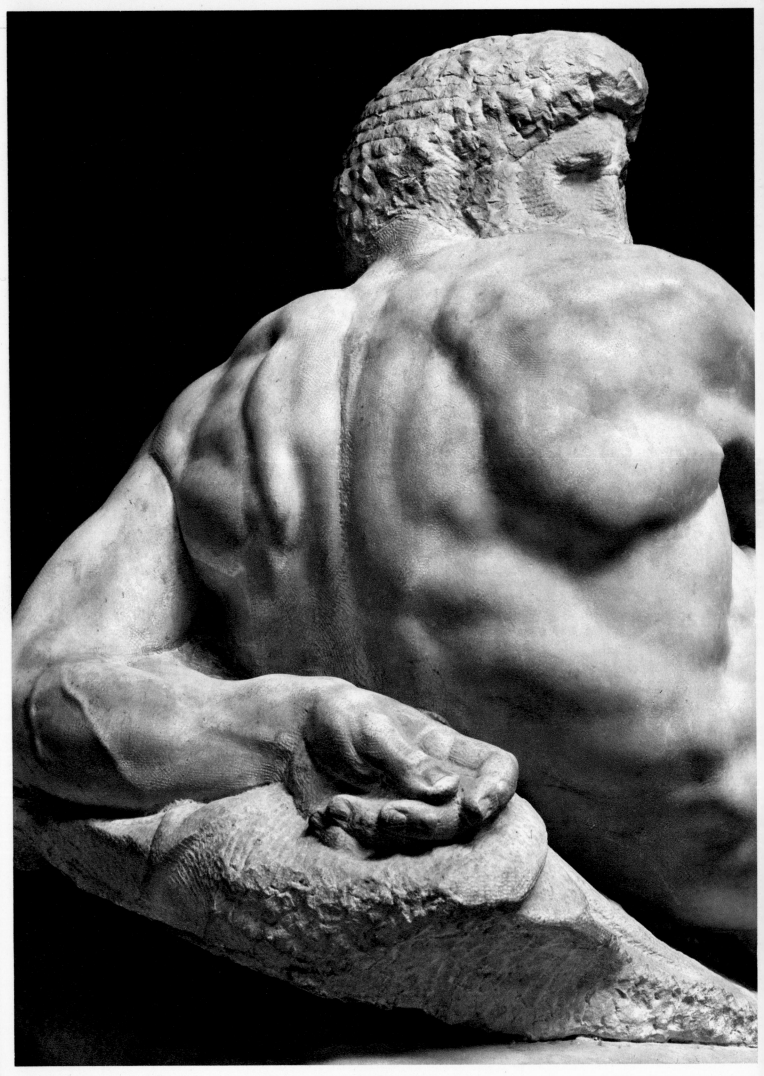

158. GIORNO. Detail of Plate 157

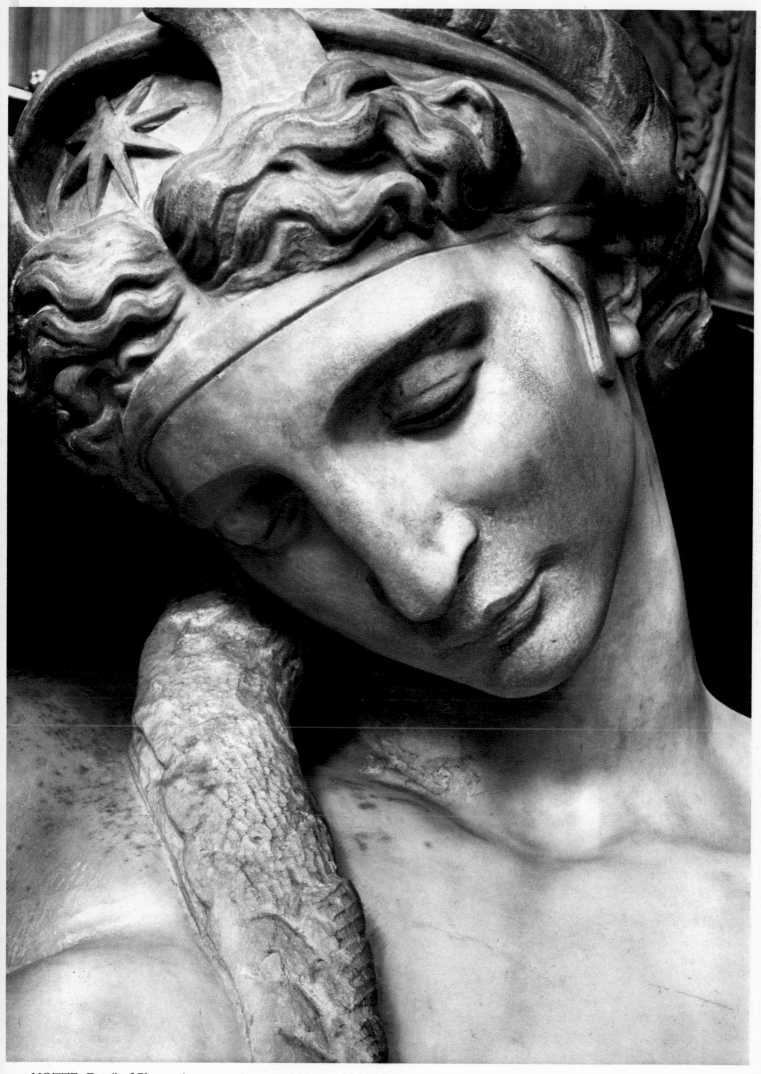

159. NOTTE. Detail of Plate 156

160. THE OWL OF LA NOTTE. Detail of Plate 156

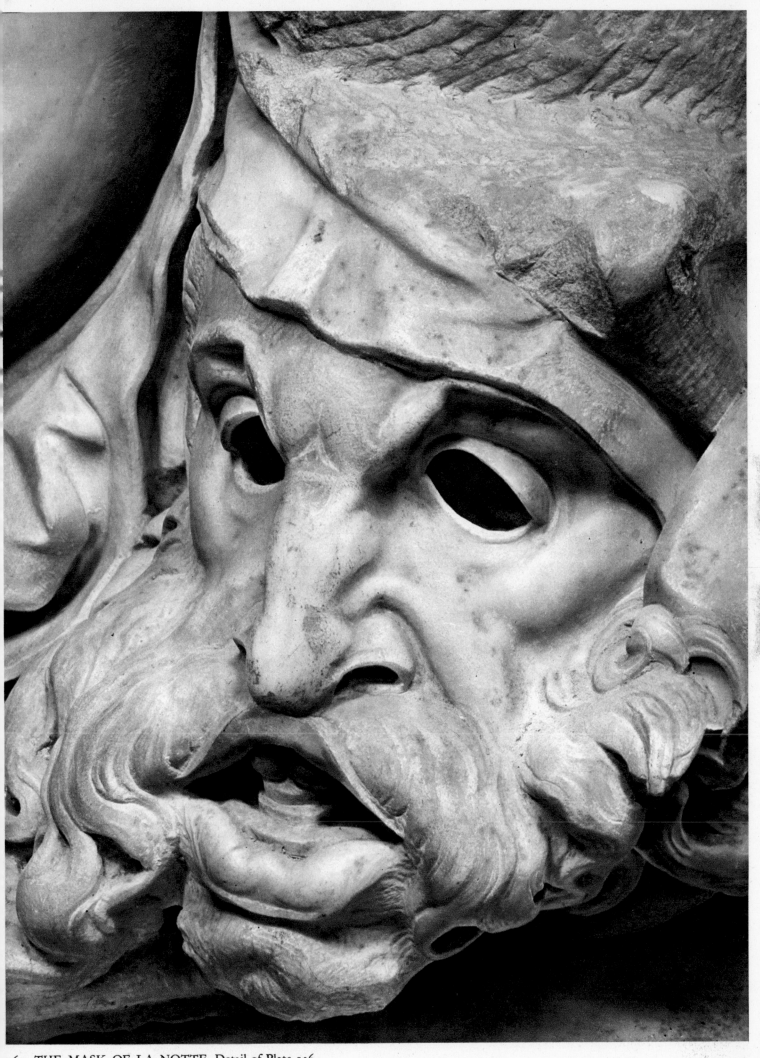

161. THE MASK OF LA NOTTE. Detail of Plate 156

162. BACK VIEWS OF "NOTTE" AND "GIORNO" (Plates 156 and 157)

163. BACK VIEW OF GIULIANO DE' MEDICI (Plate 149)

164. MADONNA AND CHILD. 1524–1534. Detail of Plate 144. Florence, Medici Chapel

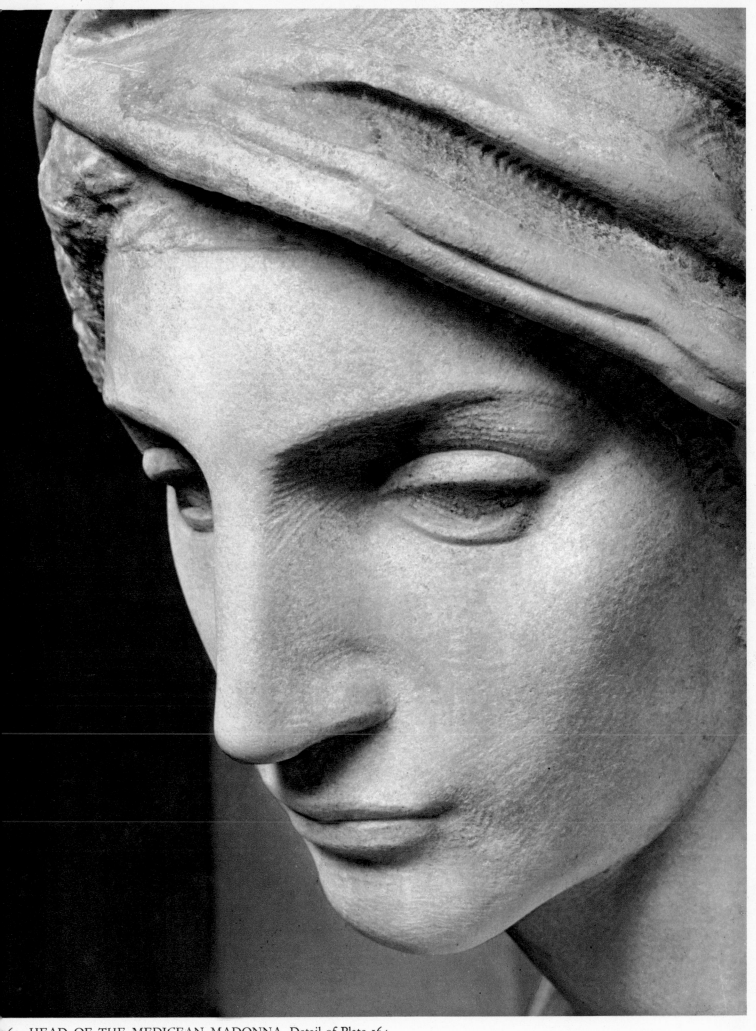

165. HEAD OF THE MEDICEAN MADONNA. Detail of Plate 164

166–167. CLAY MODEL OF A RIVER GOD. Florence, Accademia

68. CROUCHING BOY. About 1525. Leningrad, Hermitage

169. CROUCHING BOY. About 1525.
Leningrad, Hermitage

170–171. CLAY MODEL OF A VICTORY GROUP. About 1525–1528. Florence, Casa Buonarroti

172–173. VICTORY. 1525–1530. Florence, Palazzo Vecchio

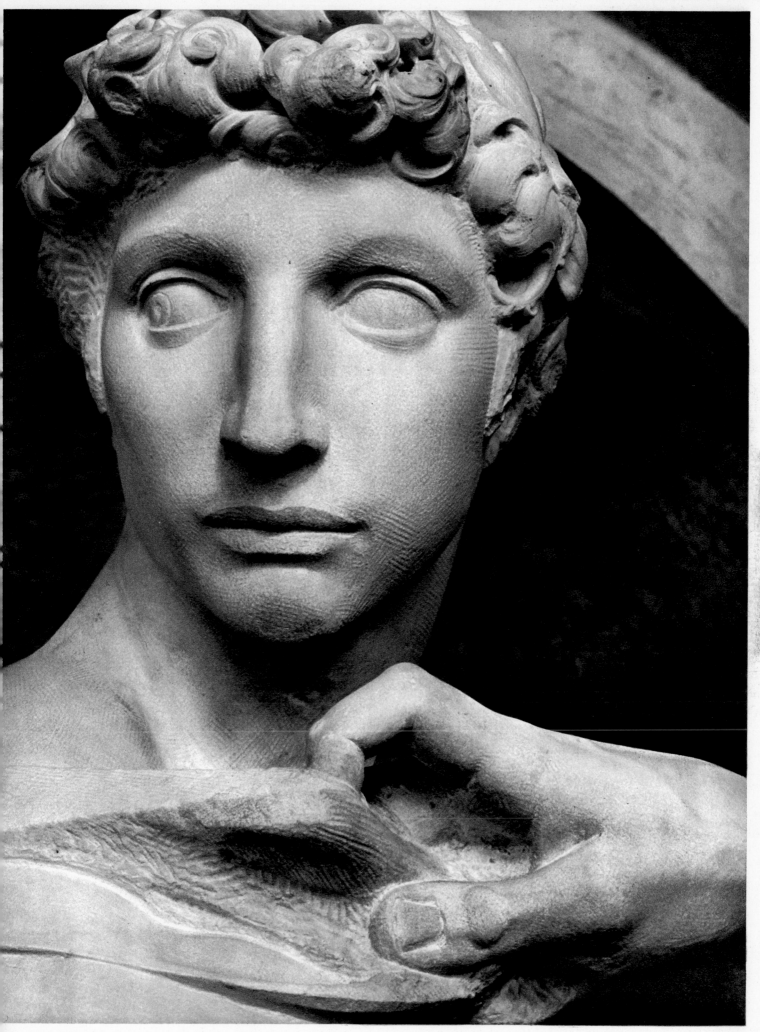

174. HEAD OF THE VICTOR. Detail of Plate 173

175-176. APOLLO. 1525-1530. Florence, Museo Nazionale del Bargello

177. APOLLO. 1525–1530. Florence, Museo Nazionale del Bargello

178. THE LAST JUDGEMENT. 1536–1541. Rome, Sistine Chapel

179. CHRIST AND THE HOLY VIRGIN. Detail of the Last Judgement, Plate 178

180. FALL OF THE DAMNED. Detail of the Last Judgement, Plate 178

181. ANGELS SOUNDING THE TRUMPETS OF DOOM. Detail of the Last Judgement, Plate 178

182. ST. BARTHOLOMEW. (Pietro Aretino holding the skin of Michelangelo.) Detail of the Last Judgement, Plate 178

183. MINOS, Prince of Hell. Detail of the Last Judgement, Plate 178

184. MICHELANGELO'S SELF-PORTRAIT. Detail of Plate 182

185. HEAD. Detail of the Last Judgement, Plate 178

186. DEMON. Detail of the Last Judgement, Plate 178

187. DEATH. Detail of the Last Judgement, Plate 178

188. THE TOMB OF POPE JULIUS II. 1505–1545. Rome, San Pietro in Vincoli. (By Michelangelo: Moses, 1516; Rachel and Leah, 1542. By Montelupo: Madonna, Prophet and Sibyl, 1542. By Tommaso di Pietro Boscoli: The figure of the Pope, 1542–1543)

189–190. RACHEL AND LEAH: Contemplative and Active Life. 1542. Detail of Plate 188. Rome, San Pietro in Vincoli

191. BRUTUS. About 1543. Florence, Museo Nazionale del Bargello

192. BRUTUS. Detail of Plate 191

193. THE CONVERSION OF SAINT PAUL. Fresco, 1542–1545. Rome, Vatican, Cappella Paolina

THE CRUCIFIXION OF SAINT PETER. Fresco, 1546–1550. Rome, Vatican, Cappella Paolina

195. CONVERSION OF SAINT PAUL. Detail of Plate 193

196. CONVERSION OF SAINT PAUL. Detail of Plate 193

197. CRUCIFIXION OF SAINT PETER. Detail of Plate 194

198. CRUCIFIXION OF SAINT PETER. Detail of Plate 194

CRUCIFIXION OF SAINT PETER. Detail of Plate 194

CONVERSION OF SAINT PAUL. Detail of Plate 193

CRUCIFIXION OF SAINT PETER. Detail of Plate 194

200. MICHELANGELO'S PLAN FOR THE PIAZZA OF THE CAPITOL IN ROME. 1546.
   After the etching by Étienne du Pérac (1569)

201. PALAZZO DEI CONSERVATORI, ROME. Finished four years after Michelangelo's death, from his designs of 1546

202. PALAZZO DEL SENATORE, ROME. Finished in 1598, partially after Michelangelo's design

203. THE OUTSIDE STEPS OF THE PALAZZO DEL SENATORE. Designed by Michelangelo, about 1546

204. PALAZZO FARNESE, ROME. Begun by Antonio da Sangallo the Younger, and continued after his death (1546) by Michelangelo, who designed the large window over the door, the windows of the upper storey and the cornice

205. THE COURTYARD OF THE PALAZZO FARNESE, from designs by Antonio da Sangallo the Younger. The upper storey designed by Michelangelo, about 1547–1550

206. CORNICE OF THE PALAZZO FARNESE. Designed by Michelangelo in 1547

207. PALAZZO FARNESE. The small windows designed by Antonio da Sangallo the Younger (about 1530); the large coat-of-arms and the centre window designed by Michelangelo (about 1550)

208. PALAZZO FARNESE. Window in the upper storey of the courtyard. About 1550

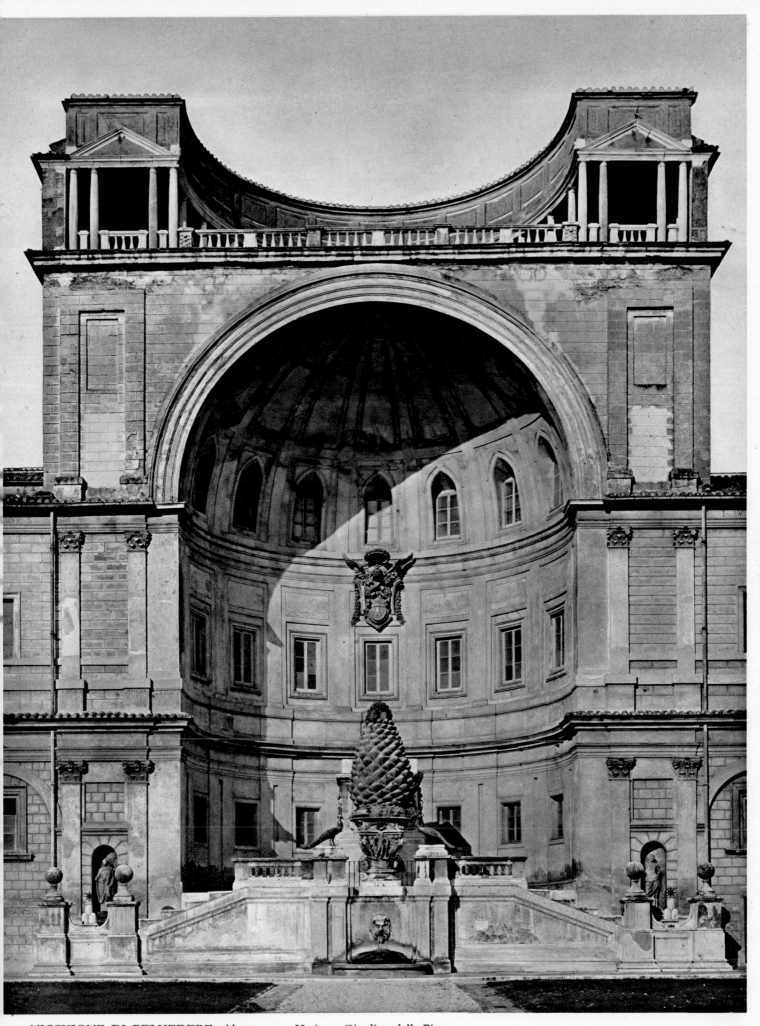

209. NICCHIONE DI BELVEDERE. About 1550. Vatican, Giardino della Pigna

210. PIETÀ. About 1548–1555. Florence, Duomo

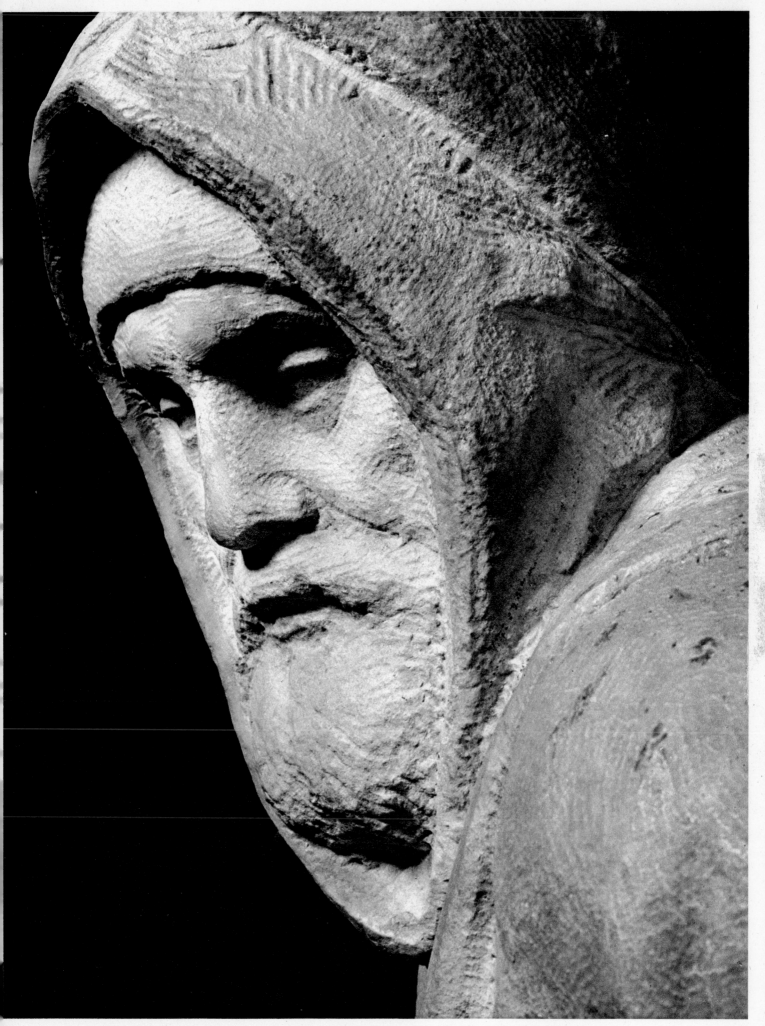

211. MICHELANGELO'S SELF-PORTRAIT AT THE AGE OF ABOUT EIGHTY. Detail of Plate 210

212. THE FLORENTINE PIETÀ. Detail of Plate 210

213. THE PALESTRINA PIETÀ. (By Michelangelo and a follower.) About 1556. Florence, Accademia

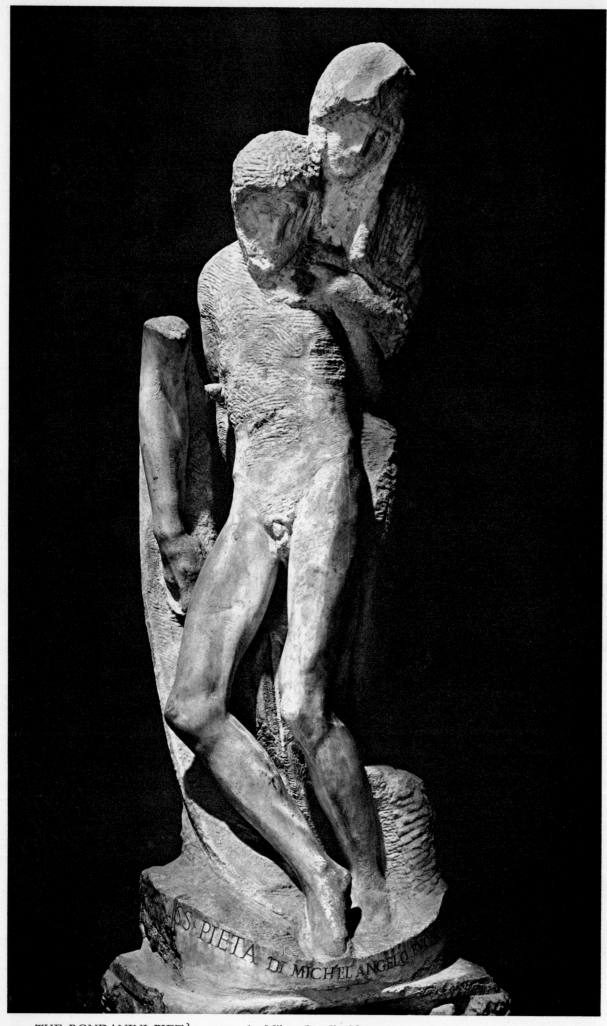

214. THE RONDANINI PIETÀ. 1555-1564. Milan, Castello Sforzesco

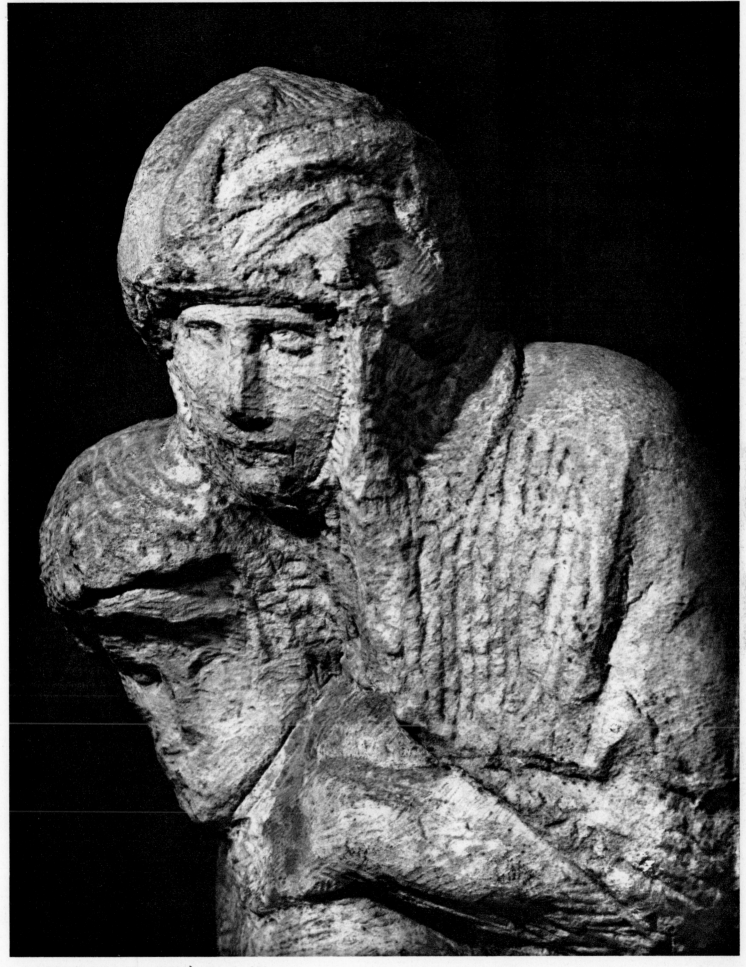

215. THE RONDANINI PIETÀ. Detail of Plate 214

216. PORTA PIA, ROME. From Michelangelo's design, 1561–1564. (The coat of arms of Pius IV by Jacomo del Duca, 1562; the centre top-piece added in 1853)

217. PORTA PIA, ROME. Detail of Plate 216

218-219. ST. PETER'S, ROME. 1546-1564

220. ST. PETER'S, ROME. Detail of the southern apse

221. ST. PETER'S, ROME. One of the niches

222. ST. PETER'S, ROME. One of the niches

223. WOODEN MODEL FOR THE CUPOLA OF ST. PETER'S. 1558–1561. Rome, Museo Petriano.
(Michelangelo's model, partially altered by Giacomo della Porta and Luigi Vanvitelli)

APPENDIX

MODELS: MICHELANGELO'S SKETCHES
IN WAX AND CLAY

LOST WORKS

ATTRIBUTIONS

MODELS IN WAX AND CLAY

Only two models appear at present to be *generally* accepted as Michelangelo's own work, both of the same period and both in clay: the large *River God* (Plate 166), and the *Victory Group* (Plate 170). A. Gottschewski was the first to recognize the River God as an original model by Michelangelo.[1] Hildebrand, Fabriczy, Schottmüller, Wölfflin and Tolnay agreed with him, but neither Frey, nor Popp, who attributed this model to Ammanati. J. Wilde has proved[2] that it is now in an incorrect position and quoted old reproductions showing how it was originally placed; in the present volume two hitherto unknown examples are added (Plate III-e, f).

The small model of a *Victory Group* (Plate 170) was accepted as genuine[3] by Bode, Fabriczy, Thode, Grünwald, Wilde, Panofsky and Tolnay. This attribution went, as far as I know, uncontradicted and we can therefore take the *Victory Group* as a starting point for the consideration of other models.

First I shall count up those models which, though not accepted by Tolnay, are of very high quality and have the opinions of great critics in their favour. (1) Wax sketch for the *Young Giant* (Plate 128) in the Victoria and Albert Museum (Plate I-b). This is the only model accepted by Berenson (*Italian Pictures*, 1932, p. 363); also by Thode, Fabriczy, Brinckmann, and by Laux (1943). (2) Clay sketch of a *Victoria*, Casa Buonarroti (Plate I-a). Accepted by Thode, Bode, Fabriczy and Popp. Knapp (*Michelangelo*, Munich, 1923, p. 48) compares it rightly to the *Victory Group* (Plate 170); it is of (relatively) the same size and the same material, and the technique is identical. (3) Clay sketch for a *Giant* (Plate I-e), accepted by Laux and others. Two torsos, one in the Casa Buonarroti and the other in the British Museum, formerly also in the Casa Buonarroti (Plate I-f, g), are of equal quality as the sketch for a *Giant* and I can therefore see no reason why they should be rejected.

The two wax sketches of *Nude Youths* (Plate I-c, d) offer a more complicated problem. Both statuettes are modelled in wax (see note 3), but they are not of identical technique. Neither are they connected with the marble or the bronze David, as was thought before, and Fabriczy has already suggested that the one model (Plate I-d) should be regarded as possibly a sketch for a figure of the Julius monument; the same was suggested by Thode concerning the other model (Plate I-c). However, I feel doubtful about Plate I-c, and am only inclined to con-

sider Plate I-d an original on the assumption that the surface of the wax has suffered and has been restored. There is also, I should think, a difference in date between the two: the first model (I-c) is of about 1513, the second (I-d) of about 1525-30.

All these models are connected with the Julius monument; the group to be discussed now consists of models for the Medici tombs. Here we have only three statuettes which are, with some authority, ascribed to the master. One of them is a slight wax sketch for *Crepuscolo* (Plate III-d), published as authentic by Sir Charles Holmes.[4] This spirited little sketch was formerly in the Casa Buonarroti. From the Casa Piccolomini in Siena came two fine large terracotta models[5] to the collection of Dr. Alejandro Pietri in Caracas, Venezuela (Plate V). Leo Planiscig, Evelyn Sandberg-Vavalà and Odoardo Giglioli have declared them to be genuine works of Michelangelo. They make a favourable impression, particularly as the position of the limbs of the terracotta figures is not exactly the same as that of the finished statues, and as the models contain richer detail. In fact, old drawings, certainly done from the models and not from the statues,[6] show the same differences.

The study of drawings by artists of the sixteenth and seventeenth centuries reproducing Michelangelo models is indeed instructive. Tintoretto owned a large number of such models, some probably originals, others only copies, and used them for studies. One set of these models was of large size, and of 'gesso', as Vasari tells us (ed. Milanesi, VII, p. 63), whereas others, which we know only from his drawings, were apparently originals.[7] The 'model' of *Giuliano* in Edinburgh is no doubt an imitation inspired by the finished statue (Plate II-d); how Michelangelo's sketch for *Giuliano* looked we learn from a Tintoretto drawing (Plate II-c). His drawing after the *Giorno* (Plate III-b), on the other hand, is probably after Daniele da Volterra's gesso copy – the face is as coarse and unfinished as that of the statue. To make use of further material, a manneristic drawing in the Uffizi (Plate III-a) cannot have been done after the statue in the Medici Chapel, because it shows the figure in positions, seen from the back and from the left, as one could not possibly see it in the Medici Chapel (cf. Plate 157). There were, however, also smaller copies available to the draughtsman of that period, of which quite a number of replicas have come down to us, e.g. the *Four Allegories* by Vincenzo Danti (1573, plaster; now in the Accademia, Perugia), or another set by Tribolo (terracotta; one of the figures repr. Plate III-c). Out of this set Vasari owned the *Notte*, but this is now lost. A bronze of the *Thief on the Cross*, which I believe to have been cast from a wax model by Michelangelo (Plate II-b), can be compared to

---

[1] In 'Munich Yearbook', I, 1906, p. 43 f.; and in 'Revista d'arte', IV, 1906, p. 73 f.

[2] In 'Belvedere,' Vienna, 1927, p. 143.

[3] In this case it can be shown how carelessly critics on the whole are dealing with the models, accepting and rejecting them, guided by some vague feelings and often without examination. Knapp (*Michelangelo*, KdK VII, 5th ed., 1924) illustrates this model on p. 166 and calls it 'stucco'; on p. 185 he calls it 'wax' and 'doubtful'. To give another example of the same unconcern, Tolnay (copying the mistake from a score of earlier critics) calls the terracotta statuette of *Aurora* in the Victoria and Albert Museum 'Notte' (*The Medici Chapel*, by C. de Tolnay, 1948, p. 155, note 7), and the sketch of a *Nude Youth* (Plate I-d), which he discusses at great length (I, p. 231 f.), 'red terracotta', although it is brown wax. (The fact that the figure is indeed wax and not terracotta has now been checked at my instigation by the restorer employed by the Casa Buonarroti and by Dr. E. Ruhmer.) Mistakes of this nature made by good critics show how little they are interested in the models, which certainly deserve greater attention.

[4] For references to the literature on this and the following pieces, see Bibliography, section X, p. 227 of this volume.

[5] These are the only models here discussed which I have not seen in the original.

[6] For instance, a mannerist drawing after the *Aurora* in the Uffizi (phot. Brogi 17754).

[7] Detlev Freiherr von Hadeln, *Zeichnungen des Giacomo Tintoretto*, Berlin, 1922. – Tietze, *The Drawings of the Venetian Painters*, New York, 1944, pp. 268-304. – W. Paesler, in 'Munich Yearbook', new series X, 1933. – Tolnay, III, 156, with references to Ridolfi and other old authors.

a similar drawing by a pupil of Michelangelo (Plate II–a), almost certainly drawn from a similar model.

One could give a long list of lost Michelangelo models. There were, e.g., the clay models he made for the figures of *Cosmas* and *Damian* (Plate IV–c, d), parts of which were owned by Vasari; there was a model of *Hercules and Antaeus* (cf. Plate XIII–g) which Michelangelo gave to Leone Leoni; there was a model for the left leg of *Giorno* which was in the possession of Alessandro Vittoria at Bologna (1563); there were the wax sketches Michelangelo made in 1517 for the figures on the wooden model for the Lorenzo façade; there was a small wax head, sent to Pietro Aretino in 1536, and a wax model for a bronze horse a year later. There is mention of other models, such as two boxes full of them, which Michelangelo gave to Antonio Mini in 1531, or the four models which were stolen in 1529, when Michelangelo's Florentine studio was broken into. All those models are apparently lost, and of the many that are shown in Dresden, Paris, Ferrara and elsewhere, only the few discussed above are genuine and even those are not generally accepted.

LOST WORKS OF MICHELANGELO

I. SCULPTURE. The first work of Michelangelo's mentioned by Condivi is the *Head of a Faun*. The artist was fourteen years old when he made it. Attempts have been made to identify as this work a mask in the Museo Nazionale, Florence, but this has since been recognized as the work of a decadent seventeenth-century master. The *Faun* has disappeared, but there is perhaps a reproduction of it in a fresco in Palazzo Pitti (Plate XIII–d). The *Wooden Crucifix*, which Michelangelo made when he was about seventeen for the Prior of Santo Spirito in Florence, has also been lost; Thode believed that he had rediscovered it in a mediocre work there. Likewise lost is the *Statue of Hercules* which passed from the Palazzo Strozzi into the possession of the King of France; nothing has been heard of it since 1713. Michelangelo was seventeen when he made this statue, which was a little larger than the 'Dying Captive' in the Louvre. As regards the *Giovannino*, or youthful St John, which Michelangelo made when he was twenty (formerly in the possession of Botticelli's patron, Lorenzo di Pierfrancesco de' Medici), Bode believed that he had rediscovered it, and Thode, Justi and Frey supported Bode's claim. Wickhoff, Wölfflin, Knapp and Mackowsky rightly rejected it and Grünwald suggests that this marble statue (now in the Berlin Museum) is the work of the manneristic Domenico Pieratti, though his grounds for this attribution are not convincing; Wölfflin suggested the Neapolitan artist Girolamo Santacroce, and Carlo Gamba thought of Silvio Cosini, one of Michelangelo's assistants. M. Gomez-Moreno (1931) found a statue in the Salvador chapel at Ubeda which he identified and published as Michelangelo's rediscovered Giovannino; Valentiner (1938) proclaimed however that an equally indifferent statue in the Morgan Library was the Giovannino. It has rightly been suggested that the St John of the Manchester Madonna might be a reproduction of this lost statue (Plate XIII–e). Condivi mentions two *Statues of Cupid* executed by Michelangelo between his return from Bologna and the time when he was working on the Bacchus (i.e. about 1496). The first version represented a *Sleeping Cupid* and was sold by the Roman dealer Baldassare del Milanese to Cardinal Riario as a genuine antique, but was thus a bogus antique. The statue came later into the possession of Cesare Borgia and then into that of Isabella d'Este, Margravine of Mantua. The Anonimo Morelliano mentions a sleeping Cupid in the house of Pietro Bembo at Padua, 'different from the copy belonging to the Duchess Isabella d'Este of Mantua'. Konrad Lange believed that he had rediscovered this early work of Michelangelo's in an indifferent exhibit in the Turin museum. A more likely supposition is that there is a reproduction of this lost work in a painting by Giulio Romano, who worked at the Mantuan court from 1525, and another in a painting by Tintoretto, of whom we know that he collected reproductions of Michelangelo's works (see Plate XIII–a, b, c; the Borghese Gallery Cupid has been lost, but there is a copy by A. Algardi in the same gallery). In 1631 the *Sleeping Cupid* is known to have passed to the collection of King Charles I of England, but all trace of it has since been lost. The other (lost) *Cupid*, sometimes also described as *Apollo*, a standing, lifesize marble figure, was made for Jacopo Galli. The lifesize *bronze statue of David*, commissioned in 1502 by Pierre de Rohan, was sent to France in 1508 via Leghorn, but nothing has been heard of it for the last three hundred years. Two wax models, one in the Casa Buonarroti and the other in the Victoria & Albert Museum, a bronze statuette in the Louvre and another in Amsterdam, have been thought to be connected with this bronze David, but these suppositions have been disputed.[1] The only basis for the reconstruction of Michelangelo's lost *bronze David* would appear to be the drawing in the Louvre (Plate XIII–k). From this drawing it is clear that Michelangelo followed Donatello, as was expressly stipulated in the contract, but it is probable that he also borrowed certain features from Verrocchio and Bertoldo. From the end of November 1506 to the end of February 1508 Michelangelo was in Bologna, engaged in casting the over-lifesize *bronze statue of Pope Julius II*, who had just conquered the city. The first casting was a failure, as the statue emerged from the furnace only as far as the girdle, but on 9 July 1507 the second casting was finished; on 21 February 1508 the statue was erected. It was nearly ten feet high and weighed about seventeen tons. The Pope was shown seated, with St Peter's keys in his left hand and his right raised in benediction. The statue stood above the main portal of San Petronio for only three years and nine months, after which the populace of

---

[1] On the model in Florence, see Thode, III, 183; IV, 79; VI, 279; on the London model, Thode, IV, 89, VI, 283; Catalogue of Italian Sculpture in the Victoria & Albert Museum, 1932, p. 131; on the Paris statuette, Courajod, *Gazette archéologique*, X, 185, p. 77 f.; Thode, III, 180 f.; IV, 88; VI, 285; on the Amsterdam statuette, A. Pitt, *Revue d'art ancien et moderne*, 1897, 78 and 455; Thode III, 182; IV, 86 f.

Bologna rose in defence of its freedom, pulled the statue down and shattered it to pieces. From the fragments Duke Alfonso of Ferrara had a mighty cannon cast, which he ironically christened 'La Giulia'. The portrait head was preserved, as the only relic of this work of Michelangelo's, in the Duke's art gallery, but has since disappeared. The destruction of the Julius statue is the most notable loss which we have to deplore among the sculptures of Michelangelo.

It is impossible to say whether the small statue of *Christ bearing the Cross*, mentioned as 'non finita' in the inventory of Michelangelo's estate[2] dated 19 February 1564, was a design for the statue in Santa Maria sopra Minerva or perhaps a reduced replica. In any case it must have been another version, for in 1564 Daniele da Volterra described it as 'similar to the Christ in the Minerva, yet differing from it'.[3] (Cf. Thode, V, 272.)

II. PAINTING.

It is impossible to determine whether Michelangelo's copy after Schongauer's engraving of the *Temptation of St Anthony* was a coloured pen-drawing (Vasari, 1550), a painting on a small wood panel (Condivi, 1553), or merely the over-painting of an original engraving (Max Lehrs, in 'Prussian Yearbook', XII, p. 130 f.; cf. Thode IV, 4). According to Varchi (1564) Michelangelo made a painting of *Ghirlandaio and his assistants at work in Santa Maria Novella* (1489); according to Vasari it was only a drawing. Vasari also mentions a tempera painting of *St Francis receiving the Stigmata*, which a dilettante is said to have executed after a cartoon by Michelangelo and which then hung in the first chapel on the left in the church of San Pietro in Montorio, Rome. This painting has since disappeared (Thode IV, p. 50).

The greatest loss we have suffered is that of the cartoon for the *Battle of Cascina*, which Michelangelo prepared in the winter of 1504–5. This work was executed in competition with Leonardo's 'Battle of Anghiari' and was intended for the left half of a wall of the council chamber in Florence (the other half of the wall was reserved for Leonardo's Battle-piece); the execution in fresco was never begun. Fragments of this cartoon were preserved until 1635, and there are numerous copies of parts of it. The oil-painting in grisaille at Holkham Hall (Plate XIV; 30 × 52 in.) is supposed to be the most comprehensive copy. The tempera painting of *Leda and the Swan*, which Michelangelo painted in 1530, was given by him to his pupil Antonio Mini, who took it with him to France. Mini's friend Benedetto del Bene established a regular 'Leda factory' in Lyons. The picture seems to have been very popular and numerous copies are extant. In London, the National Gallery and the Royal Academy own examples. (Both copies are by Rosso Fiorentino.)

On the wall opposite the 'Last Judgement', that is to say by the entrance to the Sistine Chapel, Michelangelo was to have painted a *Fall of the Angels*, and he made several sketches for it. One of his colour-mixers afterwards executed a fresco, which was formerly in the no longer existing church of the Trinità dei Monti in Rome.

III. ARCHITECTURE.

All the models in clay and wood which Michelangelo made are lost, with the exception of the one for the cupola of St Peter's. To give two examples from the year 1559, there is no trace left of the model for the Church San Giovanni dei Fiorentini in Rome (although we know it quite well from old engravings), or of the model for the staircase of the Biblioteca Laurenziana.

The Church of Santa Maria degli Angeli alle Terme and the Sforza Chapel in Santa Maria Maggiore in Rome have so much been altered by later architects that they could be counted amongst Michelangelo's lost works.

The work on Santa Maria degli Angeli was started in 1563 and finished three years later. Pope Pius IV (1559–65) commissioned Michelangelo to transform the best

The Portal of the Sforza Chapel in Santa Maria Maggiore, Rome, designed by Michelangelo. Detail of an engraving, 1621.

---

[2] This Christ and a small Pietà were left to Michelangelo's servant, Antonio del Franzese. The inventory also mentions an unfinished statue of St Peter, which Thode (I, 487) is inclined to identify with the statue of Julius II for his monument, mentioned in a letter of 1508. This 'Papa di marmo abbozzato' has also disappeared.

[3] Varchi, in his 'Funeral Oration for Michelangelo' (*Quellenschriften für Kunstgeschichte*, Vienna, 1874, VI, 119) mentions, in addition to the Minerva Christ (Plate 75), 'another Christ, completely nude, shown turning away, which he gave to the Marchesa di Pescara'.

The Thermae of Diocletian, Tepidarium. Drawing by Giov. Antonio Dosio, about 1563. Florence, Uffizi. (Cf. Plate XI–b)

preserved part of the antique Baths of Diocletian into a church. The *tepidarium* was strengthened and two large doors opened in the shorter side. Michelangelo had the help of Jacomo del Duca (who also assisted him in the work on the Porta Pia). The engraving (Plate XI–a) shows the east side of the Thermae and the large Renaissance door, designed by Michelangelo as the main entrance into the Basilica. (This door is now walled up.) Plate XI–b shows the transept of the church in the present state, as it was rebuilt by Clemente Orlandi and Luigi Vanvitelli from 1700 to 1749. Where the High Altar is now there was, in Michelangelo's time, the main entrance (see illustration). About other alterations see Thode V, 184.

The Sforza Chapel (Plate XII–b, c) is also very much re-built. The commission to Michelangelo came from Cardinal Guido Ascanio Sforza. Most of the work was done by Michelangelo's assistant Tiberio Calcagni (who also worked on some of the figures of the Florentine Pietà, and finished the 'Brutus'); after Michelangelo's death, and the death of Calcagni (1565), Giacomo della Porta finished the Chapel in 1573. The Chapel had 'a façade within the church' with a portal designed by Michel-angelo (see illustration on p. 205), but this was removed in 1748.

ATTRIBUTIONS

I. SCULPTURE. Whereas some thirty years ago the 'contractionists' were in the lead and doubts were cast even on perfectly genuine and documented works, the 'expansionists' are now busily trying out new attributions. In the previous period all finely finished drawings of Michelangelo were rejected as copies, and at the same time also certain sculptures, such as the 'Madonna of the Stairs' (Benkard), the four unfinished 'Captives' (Hilde-brand), and the large 'River God' (Popp); it was also claimed that assistants had a large share in such works as the 'Dying Captive' of the Louvre (Brinckmann), the 'Victory Group' of the Palazzo Vecchio (Wittkower), and the Madonna of Bruges (Wölfflin). Those doubts are now only of historical interest. We must however be grateful to the same critics for discarding from the œuvre of Michel-angelo a number of other sculptures that had been wrongly attributed to him for a long time: the 'Head of a Faun' in the Bargello, the 'Bronze Apollo' in the Louvre, the marble relief of 'Apollo and Marsyas' in the Baron Liphardt Collection (now in the Kress Collection, National Gallery of Art, Washington), the 'St Andrew relief' in the Bargello, and others that are not even worth mentioning. The best-known of these wrong attribu-tions was the 'Cupid' (or Narcissus) in the Victoria and Albert Museum, which is now generally acknowledged to be by Vincenzo Danti.[1]

None of the many new attributions put forward during the last thirty years has had much success. There was first the 'Head of a Cyclops' in the Bargello,[2] a dis-covery of Adolfo Venturi (L'Arte, 1922, p. 177 f.); and then the 'Bozzetto of a Crouching Girl' in a private collection at Munich,[3] sponsored by Kieslinger ('Prussian Yearbook)' 1928, p. 50 f.; but already doubted by Hekler in 'Wiener Jahrbuch für Kunstgeschichte', VII, 1930, p. 219). Tolnay has published twice (in 'Prussian Year-book', 1933, p. 121 f.; and 'The Youth of Michelangelo', Princeton, 1947) a relief with the coat of arms of Pope Julius II in the Museo Civico, Bologna. He suggested that this relief was originally underneath the lost bronze statue of Julius II on the façade of San Petronio. Bertini ('Michelangelo fino alla Sistina', 1945, p. 25) has already protested against this attribution. So has Thode (V, 191) against that of the pediment of Marcus Aurelius to Michelangelo, now once more attributed to him by Armando Schiavo (1949) and Tolnay (1951). A few more unsuccessful discoveries are mentioned in the foregoing note on the Lost Works. In Giovanni Papini's 'Vita di Michelagniolo nella vita del suo tempo', 6th edition, Milan, 1951, a new crop of finds is illustrated and dis-cussed. One is the 'Head of Hercules', in the possession of a Polish sculptor in Paris; this head is supposed to be a fragment of Michelangelo's Hercules statue, which in the time of Henry IV was at Fontainebleau;[4] another find is a 'Bust of a Youth' in a private collection in Rome.[5] These two sculptures I have not seen in the original.

---

[1] The statue of a 'Crouching Boy' in the Hermitage (Plate 168) is counted amongst the workshop productions by some critics, e.g. Kriegbaum, who assume that some *garzone*, probably Tribolo, made the statue after a small model by Michelangelo. This would put the statue into the same class as the 'Cosmas' and 'Damian' of the Medici Chapel (Plates IV–c, d), which are also only after models by the master. I believe, however, that Michelangelo himself did at least the first rough work on the marble. The 'Palestrina Pietà' (Plate 213) is, by Tolnay and others, counted amongst the Apocryphal Works; it is claimed that an imitator combined here a number of Michelangelo motives (Tolnay, 'Michel-angelo', Florence, 1951, p. 265). Toesca discussed the Palestrina Pietà as a genuine work (in 'Le Arti', I, 1938–9, p. 105 f.); on this I agree, although it is obvious that great parts of the sculpture are finished by a later hand.

[2] By some unknown sculptor of the Mannerist period.

[3] Perhaps by Vincenzo Danti.

[4] Papini, p. 54. To judge from the photograph, the poor work of a provincial Roman artist, or the copy after a Hellenistic sculpture without importance. Giovanni Antonio Gori, the Florentine archeologist, thought that he possessed the small model, about 4½ in. high, for the head of Michelangelo's 'Hercules' (Thode IV, 17).

[5] Papini, opp. p. 273. This bust is a copy from Michelangelo's 'Victory' in the Palazzo Vecchio. The technique of the copyist reminds one vaguely of Raffaelle da Montelupo's 'St Damian' in the Medici Chapel, and of his 'Prophet' on the Julius Monument.

II. PAINTING. Papini's third attribution concerns a painting in Santa Maria at Marcialla, near Florence, a 'Pietà'. This fresco was attributed to Michelangelo already by some scholars of the early eighteenth century, but since then it had been justly forgotten.[6]

There is a group of paintings, not all of them by the same hand, which are at present by some writers considered as the earliest paintings by Michelangelo.[7] Here is a complete list:

(1) *Madonna with Child and St John in a Landscape*. Dublin, National Gallery of Ireland, No. 98. Attributed to Michelangelo by Fiocco. Correctly attributed to Francesco Granacci by Mary Logan, Gronau and Berenson.

(2) *Madonna with the Candelabrum*. Vienna, Academy, No. 1134. Ascribed to Michelangelo by Adolfo Venturi and Fiocco. Rightly attributed to Antonio Mini by A. E. Popp, and to Bugiardini by Berenson.

(3) *Madonna with Child and St John*. Florence, Conte Contini Bonacossi (formerly in a private collection in London). Fiocco's attribution. By Antonio Mini.

(4) *Madonna and Child*. Private collection, Baden near Zurich. Fiocco's attribution. By Antonio Mini.

(5) *Madonna and Child*. Unknown private collection. Fiocco's attribution ('Rivista d'arte', XXVI, 1950, p. 149). By Antonio Mini.

(6) *The Manchester Madonna*. London, National Gallery, No. 809 (Plate XV–a). Attributed to Michelangelo by Toesca (1934), Kenneth Clark (1938), Fiocco and Longhi (1944), Bertini (1945). Not by Michelangelo according to Wölfflin, Berenson, Frizzoni, Adolfo Venturi, Popp, Tolnay. This and the following two paintings are of a much higher quality than the five mentioned above; all three are apparently by the same anonymous master.

(7) *The Entombment*. London, National Gallery, No. 790 (Plate XV–b). Attributed to Michelangelo by Fiocco, Longhi, Kenneth Clark, Toesca, Bertini; but not by Wölfflin, Berenson, Popp, Baumgart, Antal. By the 'Master of the Manchester Madonna'.

(8) *St John the Evangelist*. Basle, private collection. $20\frac{1}{2} \times 21\frac{1}{2}$ in. (Plate XVI). Attributed to Michelangelo by Longhi, Fiocco, Nicodemi and Magugliani (1952). By the 'Master of the Manchester Madonna'.

The last three pictures are illustrated in the present volume, being the best of the whole group. For illustrations of the others see the articles listed in footnote 7; three of them are also reproduced in Tolnay, 'Michelangelo', I, Figs. 276, 277, 279. The 'Master of the Manchester Madonna' is, I feel sure, a Florentine painter influenced by Granacci and Bugiardini; between 1516 and 1534 he was inspired by Michelangelo, and probably worked in his studio, not necessarily as a painter. A large number of drawings can also be attributed to this anonymous minor master.

---

[6] Papini, pp. 73–74, and opp. 53. Rather in the manner of Jacopo del Sellaio. According to Stendhal (*Rome, Naples et Florence*; paragraph dated 25 October 1816), the Italians attributed at one time even the designs of their tarot cards to Michelangelo!

[7] G. Fiocco, *La data di nascita di Francesco Granacci e un'ipotesi Michelangiolesca*, in 'Rivista d'arte', serie II, anno II, 1930, p. 193 f.; anno III, 1931, p. 109 f., 385 f. *Un'altra pittura giovanile di Michelangelo*, in 'Critica d'arte', anno II, 1937, fasc. X, p. 172 f. – *Sull'inizio pittorico di Michelangelo*, in 'Le Arti', anno IV, 1941, p. 5 f. – *Primizio di Michelangelo*, in 'Rivista d'arte', XXVI, 1950, p. 149 f. – R. Longhi, *A proposito dell'inizio pittorico di Michelangelo*, in 'Le Arti', anno IV, 1941, p. 136. – Cf. A. E. Popp, *Garzoni*, in 'Belvedere', VIII, 1925, p. 6 f. – L. Magugliani, in 'Annali', I, 1952, p. 20 f. and II, no. 1, February 1953.

The Piazza of the Capitol in Rome, about 1546–48,
with the outside steps of the Palazzo Senatorio, designed by Michelangelo, in the centre,
and the equestrian monument of Marcus Aurelius in front
(the pediment of which is wrongly ascribed to Michelangelo).
Anonymous engraving.

SOURCES OF PHOTOGRAPHS

THE PHOTOGRAPHS FOR PLATES I, 3–7, 9–10, 12–21, 29–33, 117–33, 135, 150–1, 154–5, 158–61, 165, 172–6, 189–92 AND 210–2 HAVE BEEN TAKEN BY ILSE SCHNEIDER-LENGYEL, THOSE FOR PLATES 188, 209 AND 214 BY A. VASARI OF ROME. FOR THE REMAINING PLATES WE HAVE USED STANDARD PHOTOGRAPHS TAKEN BY ALINARI, FLORENCE; ANDERSON, ROME; BROGI, FLORENCE; AND THE SOVRINTENDENZA ALLE GALLERIE, FLORENCE; AND PHOTOGRAPHS SUPPLIED BY MUSEUMS. THE COLOUR PHOTOGRAPHS OF THE FRESCOES IN THE VATICAN HAVE BEEN SPECIALLY TAKEN BY MR. H. HINZ OF BASLE, AND THAT OF THE MADONNA DONI BY CLAUDIO EMMER OF MILAN.

PLATE I. *Models in clay and wax, all probably for the Julius monument.*
(a) Female statuette, for a Victory group, clay. Casa Buonarroti. (b) Dark-red wax sketch for the 'Young Giant'. London, Victoria and Albert Museum. (c) Light wax sketch for a Captive. Casa Buonarroti.

(d) Dark-brownish-red wax sketch for a Captive. Casa Buonarroti. (e) Clay sketch for a 'Giant'. Casa Buonarroti. (f) Clay sketch for a 'Giant'. Casa Buonarroti. (g) Clay sketch, repaired with wax, for a 'Giant'. British Museum.

PLATE II. *Drawings of Lost Models.* (a) Thief on the Cross (drawing by Granacci [?] after a Michelangelo model). Louvre. (b) Thief on the Cross, bronze cast from a wax model by Michelangelo. Berlin, Museum.

(c) Drawing by Tintoretto after a lost model of Giuliano de' Medici by Michelangelo. Oxford, Christ Church. (d) Wax statuette of Giuliano de' Medici, by an imitator of Michelangelo. Edinburgh.

PLATE III. *The Problem of the Models for the Medici Chapel.* (a) Studies of a Florentine Mannerist after a lost model for Michelangelo's 'Giorno'. Uffizi. (b) Drawing by Tintoretto after a lost model for 'Giorno'. Oxford, Christ Church. (c) Terracotta copy of the 'Giorno' by Tribolo. Florence, Bargello. (d) Wax sketch for the 'Crepuscolo' by Michelangelo. British Museum. (e) Detail of a drawing by Joseph Heintz, about 1592, after a model by Michelangelo for a 'River God'. Vienna, Albertina. (f) Detail of a drawing by Pierino da Vinci, about 1540, after a model by Michelangelo for a 'River God'. London, Victor Koch Collection.

PLATE IV. *Designs and Models for the Medici Chapel*. (a) The Lantern on the Cupola of the Medici Chapel, c. 1521, designed by Michelangelo. (b) Candelabrum in the Medici Chapel. Designed by Michelangelo.

(c) St. Cosmas, by Giovanni Montorsoli; and (d) St. Damian, by Raffaello da Montelupo, after models by Michelangelo. Florence, Medici Chapel.

PLATE V. Terracotta models of 'Notte' and 'Aurora'. Caracas, Venezuela, Dr. Alejandro Pietri Collection.
(Attributed to Michelangelo by Planiscig and Giglioli.)

a

PLATE VI. (a) Wooden model for the Lorenzo façade. Casa Buonarroti.
(Baccio d'Agnolo's model of 1516 ? or a reduced version of Pietro Urbano's model of 1517 ?).

b   PLATE VI. (b) Windows on the outside of the Biblioteca Laurenziana, Florence.

a

c

PLATE VII. (a) The Reading Room of the Biblioteca Laurenziana, Florence. (b) Detail from the pavement of the Reading Room, by Tribolo and Sante Buglioni, 1552–1553, after a design by Michelangelo of 1524. (c) Detail from the carved ceiling of the Reading Room, by Battista del Tasso and Antonio Carota, 1534, from a design by Michelangelo.

a

b

c

d

e

f

b

d

PLATE VIII. (a) and (b) Reliefs carved in wood, on the benches in the Reading Room of the Biblioteca Laurenziana, by Battista del Cinque and Ciappino, 1534, after sketches by Michelangelo. (c–f) The four ornamental reliefs on the front of the Julius monument, by Antonio del Pontasieve, about 1513, after drawings by Michelangelo of 1506.

PLATE IX. (a) and (b) Ornaments over the niches of Rachel and Leah. (c) and (d) The two ornamental reliefs inside the recess for the Moses statue. By Antonio del Pontasieve, after designs by Michelangelo.

a

b

PLATE X. Michelangelo's designs for St. Peter's, engravings by Étienne du Pérac, 1569. Vienna, Albertina.

PLATE XI. (a) The Thermae of Diocletian, converted into the Church of Santa Maria degli Angeli by Michelangelo, 1563–1566. (In the centre, the old portal designed by Michelangelo is partially visible.) Detail of an engraving by Alò Giavannoli, about 1610. Rome, Biblioteca Angelica. (b) The transept of Santa Maria degli Angeli, Rome, in the present state, rebuilt by Vanvitelli in 1749.

a

b

c

PLATE XII. (a) The Tomb of Cecchino Bracci, by Francesco Urbino, from a design by Michelangelo, 1545. Rome, Santa Maria in Araceli.

(b) and (c) The Sforza Chapel (Santa Maria Maggiore, Rome) by Tiberio Calcagni, about 1559–1565, finished by Giacomo della Porta, 1573.

PLATE XIII. *Lost Sculptures*. (a–c) Michelangelo's lost work 'Sleeping Cupid'. (a) The antique model, after an engraving in Montfaucon's 'L'Antiquité expliquée', 1720. (b) Detail from Tintoretto's 'Mars and Venus', c. 1545, Munich, Ältere Pinakothek. (c) Detail from Giulio Romano's 'The Infancy of Jupiter', c. 1535, London, National Gallery. (d) Michelangelo's lost work 'Head of a Faun'. Detail from a fresco by Ottavio Vannini in the Palazzo Pitti at Florence, painted about 1640. (e) The lost 'Giovannino'. Detail of a drawing by Michelangelo (Louvre), used by the Master of the Manchester Madonna (cf. Plate XV–a). (f) and (g) Sketches for lost models (about 1525; British Museum, BB.1688 and 1490), 'Hercules and Cacus' and 'Hercules and Antaeus'. (h–k) The lost 'Bronze David'. (h) Donatello's bronze David, c. 1440. Florence, Bargello. (i) Bronze statuette after a model for the Martelli David, sometimes attributed to Donatello, Berlin, Museum. (j) Bronze statuette of a David in the Rijksmuseum, Amsterdam, c. 1530. (k) Detail of a Michelangelo drawing for the Bronze David (1502; Louvre).

PLATE XIV. Bastiano, called Aristotile da Sangallo: Copy after Michelangelo's cartoon for the Battle of Cascina. Holkham Hall, Earl of Leicester.

PLATE XV. 'The Master of the Manchester Madonna': Two paintings in the National Gallery, London. (a) Madonna and Child, with St. John. (b) Entombment.

(Attributed by Fiocco, Longhi, Toesca, Sir Kenneth Clark, Bertini, d'Ancona; but not by Wölfflin, Berenson, A. Venturi, Popp, Antal, Baumgart, Tolnay, and the author of the present book.)

PLATE XVI. St. John the Evangelist in a Landscape. Private Collection. (Attributed to Michelangelo by Longhi, Fiocco, Nicodemi and Magugliani.)
By the same Master as the two paintings reproduced on Plate XV.

BIBLIOGRAPHY
AND
INDEX TO THE PLATES

BIBLIOGRAPHY

The following list is intentionally kept concise, in order to help the student to find the most important titles first. There is a complete Michelangelo Bibliography in Vols. I and VIII of the *Romische Forschungen* of the Biblioteca Hertziana in Rome – *Michelangelo-Bibliographie* by E. Steinmann and R. Wittkower (1927), and a continuation by H. W. Schmidt in *Michelangelo im Spiegel seiner Zeit* (1930). For publications after 1930, see *Art Index*, New York, 1929 f., and Cherubelli, *Supplemento alla bibliografia michelangiolesca, 1931-42* (in 'Michelangelo Buonarroti nel IV centenario del Giudizio Universale'), Florence, 1942; a few additions in E. Aeschlimann, *Bibliografia del Libro d'arte italiano 1940-52*, Rome, 1952.

I. THE OLD BIOGRAPHIES · DOCUMENTS · LETTERS

The two versions of the Michelangelo biography by Vasari (1550 and 1568) and the biography by Condivi are contained in a critical edition by Karl Frey, *Le vite di Michelagniolo Buonarroti scritte da Giorgio Vasari e da Ascanio Condivi*, Berlin, 1887. The first Vasari biography is separately available in a reprint by Corrado Ricci (Milan, 1927). There are three recent reprints of the Condivi biography, the best by Paolo d'Ancona (Milan, 1928). Many of the documents are to be found in Aurelio Gotti, *Vita di Michelangelo*, Florence, 1876; others in G. Gaye, *Carteggio inedito d'artisti*, 3 vols., Florence, 1839-40. – The only edition of Michelangelo's letters is still G. Milanesi, *Le lettere di Michelangelo Buonarroti*, Florence, 1875; the same editor collected Michelangelo's correspondence with Sebastiano del Piombo (*Les Correspondants de Michel-Ange*, I, Paris, 1890), whereas K. Frey gives a selection from all the letters addressed to the master in *Sammlung ausgewählter Briefe an Michelagniolo Buonarroti*, Berlin, 1899. The standard edition of Michelangelo's poetry is edited by K. Frey, Berlin, 1897. – There are several editions of the *Dialogues* of Francisco de Hollanda and those of Donato Giannotti, but they cannot be catalogued in this short bibliography.

II. GENERAL BOOKS ON THE LIFE AND WORK OF MICHELANGELO

Of the six volumes of Henry Thode's *Michelangelo* (Berlin, 1902-13) only vols. IV and V will prove of great value to the reader of the present book. They are published separately as 'Kritische Untersuchungen, I-II'. The sixth volume contains a catalogue of the drawings and a short list of the models. – A good survey of Michelangelo's œuvre is available in Charles de Tolnay's article in *Thieme-Becker's Künstlerlexikon*, vol. XXIV, Leipzig, 1930; another one, by Pietro Toesca, in *Enciclopedia Italiana*, vol. XXIII, pp. 165-191, Rome, 1934. – There is a corpus of illustrations, edited by F. Knapp in 'Klassiker der Kunst', vol. VII, Stuttgart, 1924, containing too much and too little; and a fat volume by Charles de Tolnay, Florence, 1951, also incomplete; for instance, of the twelve Prophets and Sibyls of the Sistine Ceiling, this volume shows only four, and of the twenty nude Youths only two. Though not complete, the book is of great value owing to some illustrative material not available elsewhere. – The best edition of the *Sculptures* is by F. Kriegbaum, Berlin, 1940. – For a full list of separate essays, see the Bibliographies above; the best of those essays are only published in German, as Carl Justi's *Beiträge*, Berlin, 1900 and 1909; A. Grünwald's *Florentiner Studien*, Dresden, 1920; and Adolf Hildebrand's *Gesammelte Aufsätze*, Strasbourg, 1915. There is no really good biography of Michelangelo available in English, as the popular book by Romain Rolland (Paris, 1914), of which there is a translation, is rather misleading (see E. Panofsky, *Michelangelo-Literatur*, 1914-22, in 'Jahrbuch für Kunstgeschichte', I, Vienna, 1923) and J. A. Symonds's often reprinted *Life and Works of Michelangelo Buonarroti* (London, 1893) is definitely out of date. Herman Grimm's *Life of Michelangelo*, although first published thirty years earlier, is perhaps more satisfactory; there exists a good English translation of this book.

III. THE EARLY WORKS OF MICHELANGELO

Charles de Tolnay's *The Youth of Michelangelo*, 2nd ed., Princeton, 1947, containing full bibliographical references; some more in Aldo Bertini's *Michelangelo fino alla Sistina*, 2nd ed., Turin, 1945. The Piccolomini statuettes were re-assessed by Friedrich Kriegbaum, *Le Statue di Michelangelo nell'Altare dei Piccolomini a Siena* (in 'Michelangelo Buonarroti nel IV centenario del Giudizio Universale'), Florence, 1942; and by W. R. Valentiner, *Michelangelo's Statues on the Piccolomini Altar in Siena* (in 'Art Quarterly', 1942; reprinted in *Studies of Italian Renaissance Sculpture*, London, 1950).

IV. THE SISTINE CEILING FRESCOES

Ernst Steinmann, *Die Sixtinische Kapelle*, Vol. II, Munich, 1905. (On pp. 687 f. the Documents, edited by H. Pogatscher.) – Charles de Tolnay, *The Sistine Ceiling*, Princeton, 1945. (With references to further literature – by Wölfflin, Justi, Panofsky, Biagetti, etc.)

V. THE TOMB OF POPE JULIUS II

Karl August Laux, *Michelangelos Juliusmonument*, Berlin, 1943. (With bibliography.) On the ornamental reliefs: Frida Schottmüller, *Michelangelo und das Ornament*, in 'Vienna Yearbook', new series, vol. II, 1928.

VI. ARCHITECTURE

Heinrich von Geymüller, *Michelangelo als Architekt* ('Architektur der Renaissance in Toskana', Vol. VIII), Munich, 1904. – Armando Schiavo, *Michelangelo Architetto*, Roma, 1949 (good plates, text in English, no bibliography). – Corrado Ricci, *Baukunst und dekorative Plastik der Hoch- und Spät-Renaissance in Italien*, Stuttgart, 1923 (340 Plates). – 'Geschichte der Neueren Baukunst', Vol. I: Jacob Burckhardt, *Geschichte der Renaissance in Italien*, 5th edition, Esslingen, 1912. – A. E. Brinckmann, *Die Baukunst des 17. und 18. Jahrhunderts in den romanischen Ländern*, Berlin, 1915–19. – Jacques Veysset, *Le Palais Farnese*, Rome, 1948. – On the cornice of the Palazzo Farnese, S. Meller in 'Prussian Yearbook', XXX, 1909, p. 1 f. – On *Santa Maria degli Angeli*, Pasquinelli, Rome, 1932 and 1935. – Dagobert Frey, *Michelangelo-Studien*, Vienna, 1920 (on the 'Nicchione di Belvedere', and other essays). – Dagobert Frey, *Eine unbeachtete Zeichnung nach dem Modell Michelangelos für die Fassade von San Lorenzo*, in 'Kunstchronik', Dec. 1922, p. 226 f. – R. Wittkower, *Zur Peterskuppel Michelangelos*, in 'Zeitschrift für Kunstgeschichte', II, 1933, p. 348 f. – The same author on *the Biblioteca Laurenziana*, in 'Art Bulletin', XVI, 1934, p. 123 f. – Charles de Tolnay, on *the façade of San Lorenzo*, in 'Gazette des Beaux-Arts', XI, 1934, p. 24 f. – The same author, on *the Libreria Laurenziana*, ib. XIV, 1935, p. 81 f. – The same author, in 'Prussian Yearbook', LI, 1930, p. 3 f., and LIII, 1932, p. 231 f.: *Beiträge zu den späten architektonischen Projekten Michelangelos*. – B. M. Apolloni, *Opere architettoniche di Michelangelo a Firenze*, Rome 1936. – V. Fasolo, *La Cappella Sforza di Michelangelo*, in 'Architettura e Arti Decorative', III, 1924, p. 433 f. – A. Michaelis, *Michelangelos Plan zum Kapitol*, in 'Zeitschrift für bildende Kunst', 1891, new series, II, p. 184 f. – Dagobert Frey's essay on the model of the Cupola of St Peter's in his *Michelangelo-Studien*, Vienna, 1920, pp. 91–136, can only be used together with the corrections noted in Erwin Panofsky's *Die Michelangelo-Literatur seit 1914*, in 'Jahrbuch für Kunstgeschichte', I, Vienna, 1923, col. 18–21. – See also Hans Rose (in H. Wölfflin's 'Renaissance und Barock', fourth edition, Munich, 1926), *Der Kuppelbau*, pp. 291–310. – Valerio Mariani, *Michelangelo e la Facciata di S. Pietro*, Rome, 1943. – Adolfo Venturi, *L'architettura del Cinquecento* ('Storia dell'arte italiana', vol. XI, parte II), Milan, 1939.

VII. THE MEDICI CHAPEL

F. Burger, *Geschichte des florentinischen Grabmals von den ältesten Zeiten bis Michelangelo*, Strasbourg, 1904. – H. Brockhaus, *Michelangelo und die Medici-Kapelle*, Leipzig, 1909. – A. E. Popp, *Die Medici-Kapelle Michelangelos*, Munich, 1922. – Charles de Tolnay, *The Medici Chapel*, Princeton, 1948. – Erwin Panofsky, *The Neoplatonic Movement and Michelangelo*, in 'Studies in Iconology', New York, 1939, pp. 129–230. – Ernst Steinmann, *Das Geheimnis der Medicigräber Michelangelos*, Leipzig, 1907.

VIII. THE LAST JUDGEMENT AND THE PAOLINA FRESCOES

D. Redig de Campos and B. Biagetti, *Il Giudizio Universale*, 2 vols., Rome, 1943. – F. Baumgart and B. Biagetti, *Die Fresken des Michelangelo in der Cappella Paolina*, Città del Vaticano, 1934. – (Same, Italian edition, Coll. 'Monumenti Vaticani di Archeologia e d'Arte', Roma, 1934.) – V. Mariani, *Gli affreschi di Michelangelo nella Cappella Paolina*, Rome, 1931 and 1932. – D. Redig de Campos, *Affreschi della Cappella Paolina in Vaticano*, Milan, 1950. – Karl Borinski, *Das Altargemälde der Sixtina* (The Last Judgement), in 'Die Rätsel Michelangelos', Munich, 1908, pp. 281–330. – D. Redig de Campos, *Fonti di Giudizio di Michelangelo* in 'Raffaello e Michelangelo, Studi di storia e d'arte', Rome, 1946. – *Studi e provvidenze per gli affreschi di Michelangelo nelle Cappelle Sistina e Paolina. Notizie ... di B. Nogara e B. Biagetti*, in 'Rendiconti della Pontificia Accademia Romana di Archeologia', IX, 1934, pp. 167–199.

IX. SOME LATE WORKS

H. von Einem, *Bemerkungen zur Florentiner Pietà*, in 'Prussian Yearbook', LXI, 1940, p. 77 f. – C. de Tolnay, *The Rondanini Pietà* in 'Burlington Magazine', LXV, 1934, p. 146. – F. Baumgart, *Die Pietà Rondanini*, in 'Prussian Yearbook', LVI, 1935, p. 47 f. – C. de Tolnay, *Michelangelo's Bust of Brutus*, in 'Burlington Magazine', LVII, 1935, p. 23 f.
For literature on Michelangelo's late works of Architecture, see under VI, above.

X. THE MODELS IN WAX AND CLAY

A. E. Popp, *Die Medicikapelle*, discusses the Edinburgh models. – F. Burger, *Studien zu Michelangelo*, 1907, p. 40 f. and J. Meier-Graefe, *Michelangelo: Die Terrakotten aus der Sammlung Hähnel*, 1924, discuss the Dresden models. – On the pieces in the British Museum, see Sir Charles Holmes, *Burlington Magazine*, XI, 1907, p. 189. – The best information on the models in the Victoria & Albert Museum is given by Sir Eric Maclagan in the 1932 catalogue, p. 127 f.; also in *Burlington Magazine*, XLIV, 1924, p. 4 f.; a few particulars in Brinckmann, *Barock-Bozzetti*. – Several terracotta models are catalogued in Cornelius von Fabriczy's *Kritisches Verzeichnis toskanischer Holz- und Tonstatuen bis zum Beginn des Cinquecento* in 'Prussian Yearbook', 1909, Beiheft, pp. 38–46. – The two terracotta models in the Pietri collection are discussed by Odoardo H. Giglioli, *Due Bozzetti inediti di Michelangelo*, Florence; and *Documenti di due bozzetti inedite*, Lugano, 1951 (with contributions by L. Planiscig, E. Sandberg-Vavalà, a.o.); also Natalia Rosi de Tariffi, in 'Periscopio', Caracas, 1952, No. 6, pp. 11–16. – Other models connected with statues of the Medici Chapel are mentioned in E. Steinmann's *Geheimnis der Medicigräber*, Leipzig, 1907; and in Julius von Schlosser's *Aus der Bildnerwerkstatt der Renaissance*, in 'Vienna Yearbook', XXXI, 1913, p. 108 f. – The terracotta sketch for a battle group ('Hercules and Cacus') in the Casa Buonarroti is discussed by J. Wilde in 'Dedalo', VIII, 1928, p. 653 f. and in 'Vienna Yearbook', 1928, p. 199 f. – H. Thode, *Michelangelo: Kritische Untersuchungen über seine Werke*, III (Vol. VI of the whole work), Berlin, 1913, pp. 265–286, gives an (incomplete) catalogue of all the models attributed to Michelangelo.

INDEX TO THE PLATES

I. ARCHITECTURE

II. PAINTINGS

III. SCULPTURES

IV. MODELS

Roman Figures refer to the Plates in the Appendix.